BATTLE EYE

A HISTORY OF AMERICAN COMBAT PHOTOGRAPHY

NORMAN B. MOYES

**Foreword by Pulitzer Prize–Winning Combat
Photographer David Hume Kennerly**

MetroBooks

MetroBooks

An Imprint of Friedman/Fairfax Publishers

Library of Congress Cataloging-in-Publication Data

Moyes, Norman B.
    Battle eye : a history of American combat photography / Norman
B. Moyes.
        p.   cm.
    Includes bibliographical references and index.
    ISBN 1-56799-287-0 (hc)
    1. War photography--United States--History. 2. United States-
-History, Military--Pictorial works.   I. Title.
TR820.6.M69   1996
779.9'973--dc20   95-51982
                                                           CIP

Editor: Tony Burgess
Art Director: Jeff Batzli
Designer: Galen Smith
Photography Director: Christopher C. Bain
Photography Editor: Colleen Branigan

Color separations by Bright Arts (Singapore) Pte. Ltd.
Printed in China by Leefung-Asco Printers Ltd.

Grateful acknowledgment is given to authors, publishers, and photographers for permission to reprint material. Every effort has been made to
determine copyright owners of photographs and of reprinted textual
material. In the case of any omissions, the Publisher will be pleased to
make suitable acknowledgments in future editions.

For bulk purchases and special sales, please contact:
Friedman/Fairfax Publishers
Attention: Sales Department
15 West 26th Street
New York, NY 10010
212/685-6610   FAX 212/685-1307

TABLE OF CONTENTS

PREFACE

In the days before photography, illustrators were eager to record war—and to give us what they thought was a glorious testament to the fighters and the leaders.

But the majority of these artists who depicted war in paintings, mosaics, tapestries, and engravings concerned themselves with the romantic concept of war and showed it as if it were only a mildly unpleasant diversion from the rigors of fox hunting and teatime.

Even the work of Roger Fenton—the man considered the first combat photographer—conveys this almost idyllic image of war. Sent to cover the Crimean War for his native England in 1855, Fenton was concerned with allaying his countrymen's fears about the care and well-being of the British soldiers. And many of his pictures, especially those showing warships in the harbor, have an unreal aura about them. Likewise, his photos of the medical tents, kitchens, weapons, and fortifications carefully avoided the fact that the soldiers shown were living through an unspeakable hell on earth.

Nonetheless, unlike the combat artists—few of whom ever witnessed war close up—Fenton, perhaps because he was enduring the dangers faced by the average soldier, was able to bring something approaching reality to his pictures.

A few years later, the situation changed. Photographers hired by Mathew Brady traveled with the Civil War armies and made what *Harper's* magazine termed "grim visages of war." For the first time, people back home found out what the term "the fallen" actually meant.

This book documents the determination, skill, and daring of combat photographers. Their experiences are documented not only by their photographs, but also by their first-person accounts of what it was like to be in the thick of the action. Sixty-seven photographers have been singled out for their unique contributions; their biographies are included in the Appendix.

The most extensive bibliography ever compiled on war photography is included so that scholars of the future will have an easier time assembling information on the subject.

The author wishes to thank the hundreds of historians and photographers who gladly gave their time and knowledge to help make this book as complete as possible.

A number need to be singled out: William Cottrell, the author's combat photography teacher at the Signal School, Fort Monmouth, New Jersey; Prof. Fred A. Demarest and Dr. Robert Root, Syracuse University; Prof. Edmund C. Arnold and Dr. David Manning White, Virginia Commonwealth University; Dr. S. J. Weissberger, Penn State University; Josephine Cobb, the National Archives; Roger Leddington, Associated Press; Ted Majeski, United Press International; Beaumont Newhall, George Eastman House; Marrion L. Mullen and Mary E. O'Hare, Syracuse University Library; Frank C. Kerr, The Chosin Few, Boston; Bill Rosmond and Bob Melhorn, Department of the Army; George Silk, Carl Mydans, and David Douglas Duncan, *Life* magazine; Cornell Capa, International Center for Photography; and Sean Callahan.

Finally, I would like to thank my editors at Michael Friedman Publishing Group, Inc.: Sharyn Rosart, Tony Burgess, Chris Bain, and Colleen Branigan, whose concern and hard work is evident in this book.

—Norman B. Moyes

FOREWORD
THE PHOTOGRAPHER IN WAR

War. The big picture show. I remember walking up and down the row of Huey helicopters that waited ominously to airlift GIs into combat. I'd pause at one, shake my head, then approach another. This ritual, an attempt to get a sense of which one wouldn't get shot down in flames, would go on for five or ten minutes until the engines coughed to life, rotor blades turning like a steam engine's wheels, slowly at first, then moving faster and faster, raising dust and a deafening whine. The soldiers piled inside the fragile birds (deathtraps, I thought) and hunkered down to be taken to their destiny. At this last possible moment, I would select a chopper and, clutching my cameras, jump aboard, my legs hanging out the door as we lifted off for another wild ride into hell.

That terrifying, exciting feeling of heading into combat is an experience shared by millions, but only a few of those millions carried cameras rather than guns. I was one of those few.

My first stab at getting into combat was in 1965. I had just graduated from a small Oregon high school. I knew there was a big world out there to shoot, but I had no idea of how to get to it or what to do if I did. Then I saw an issue of *Life* magazine that contained photographer Larry Burrows's brilliant essay, "Yankee Papa 13." Burrows was flying with a helicopter rescue unit; a member of the helicopter crew was killed during the operation, and Burrows recorded every moment on film. Seeing those photographs was the most profound moment of my life up to that point. The images conveyed a deeply moving combination of honesty, courage, and humanity. It was life in the raw and life on the line. I suddenly realized that those were the kind of pictures I wanted to take.

As an eighteen-year-old aspiring photographer the closest thing to real human drama that I'd seen was an occasional fire or car wreck. But a war? There was no way for me to comprehend what that would be like. I approached the Associated Press bureau chief in Portland, Oregon about going to Vietnam for them, but he just laughed. "You gotta make it here first," he said. Six years would pass before I did that.

In my attempt to prove myself I landed a job with United Press International and plunged head first into the business. During those years I felt like the title character in the film "Mr. Roberts," played by Henry Fonda. Mr. Roberts spends most of the Second World War on a supply ship watching the destroyers steam by him into combat. He desperately wants to be on one of them, in the middle of the action, not on the edge of it. Every time someone else at UPI got the call to battle instead of me, I would panic. What if the war ended before I could get to it? Finally, after pleading with the wire service's hierarchy so often that they hated to see me coming, they relented. And like Mr. Roberts, I finally got my chance to get into the middle of the action.

Ironically, I never did get the chance to meet my photo hero and inspiration. Two weeks before I left the U.S. for Vietnam, Burrows and three other photographers were killed when their helicopter was shot down over Laos. On board were Henri Huet of the Associated Press, Keisaburo Shimamoto of *Newsweek*, and Kent Potter of UPI, whom I was to replace in the Saigon bureau. The idea of "war photography" had abruptly become less theoretical. I was scared to death when I boarded that plane to Saigon, and I didn't feel any better when I noticed that UPI had only bought me a one-way ticket.

Who are war photographers anyway?

David Douglas Duncan, a photographer of wars, among other things, said "Anyone who believes that war photography requires much more talent than affixing oneself—leech-like in combat boots, a parasite complete with camera—to the bleeding body of war-torn humanity, knows nothing of war, or of photography. To make a cult of war photography is obscene.... To assign any sort of distinction, by classification, to any photographer who has happened to cover combat in his life is profane." If Duncan includes himself in that group, then he was one of war's most successful and prominent parasites. His pictures of World War II, Korea, and Vietnam are some of the best ever taken.

Dick Swanson, a remarkable photographer who made some haunting and compelling pictures in Vietnam, responded to Duncan by saying, "Hell, the only time I ever called myself a war photographer was when I was trying to get laid." A sense of humor is an invaluable tool for any photographer of war.

In Vietnam, each photographer on the front lines had a different reason for being there. Some went for the adventure, some to prove their manhood. Some were anti-American, others were pro-American. Some were trying to gain a reputation, while others were trying to lose one. But whatever the reason, they all had one unifying cause. They were there for the pictures. And as in any other profession, some were better than others. Horst Faas, the Associated Press photographer, won two Pulitzer Prizes, the first for his Vietnam photos, the second shared with Michel Laurent for coverage of the bayoneting spectacle after the India-Pakistan war in Dacca. He once said "there are camera users and there are photographers." Every war has had its share of camera users, but the photographers took the pictures we all remember. And many of those photographers gave their lives to take those photographs.

Michel Laurent was one of them. He had the dubious distinction of being the last photographer killed in Vietnam. The first was Robert Capa. Michel and I were friends and competitors, but we were friends first. After the end of the India-Pakistan war, which we covered for our respective wire services, we both ended up in Dacca. We waited several days for the return of Sheikh Mujibir Rahman, who would become the first president of the former East Pakistan, now called Bangladesh. The day he arrived I had come down with some ghastly bug and was running a high fever. I tried to cover the event, which culminated in a motorcade conveying the victorious Sheikh through a million cheering people in the 120-degree heat, but I couldn't do it. Michel took my cameras, shot the event for me, then gave me the film. The pictures were better than the ones he turned in. Not many years later, Michel was mortally wounded on the outskirts of Saigon as he tried to photograph the advancing North Vietnamese Army troops moving toward the city center and victory.

Another photographer who died in Vietnam was Gerard Hubert. He was one of those who were trying to lose one reputation and gain another, although I didn't find that out until after he died. Hubert worked as a freelancer for me when I was UPI photo chief in Saigon. One day he burst through the door bleeding and covered with bandages. "What happened to you?!" I exclaimed. "The VC shoot me in An Loc," he replied, handing me an envelope, "here's the film, now I must go to the hospital." Wow. Hubert, who had been decorated for saving several South Vietnamese soldiers under heavy fire, was later killed on an operation in Quang Tri. When we tried unsuccessfully to locate his relatives, we discovered that the name Hubert was a pseudonym. He was a French-Canadian on the lam from the Canadian authorities. I knew him only as a brave and dedicated photographer.

Taizo Ichinose was a camera user turned photographer. Taizo showed up on my doorstep at UPI carrying a Nikon and one phrase of English, "Have good picture." What Taizo lacked in skill or talent he more than made up for in guts and desire. His photos of the South Vietnamese in battle were some of the best I'd ever seen, and you could practically hear the gunfire and smell the fear as you looked at them. Taizo got too close to the Khmer Rouge in Cambodia and was captured by them near Angor Wat. He hasn't been seen since and is presumed dead.

Willie Vicoy was also my friend and fellow photographer. He worked with me at UPI in Vietnam. Willie was one of the most outwardly cheerful people I've ever known, but he admitted that sometimes the dead children he photographed came back on quiet nights to haunt him. Willie had so many close calls in Vietnam that he never thought he'd make it home alive. He did, though, only to die of shrapnel wounds received while covering Philippine government troops battling communist guerrillas in Cagayan Province in 1986. He was 45. Philippine President Corazon Aquino said of him, "For a man whose life has been meaningful, death cannot be meaningless...he did not fall in the line of duty, but rather he died venturing beyond it." Those words summed up not only Willie's death, but also those of many others who fell covering combat.

And what about the soldiers' attitude toward the photographers? Invariably I was asked the same question in one form or another by awestruck GIs who, upon seeing this bearded, camera-packing, fedora-wearing, fatigue-clad civilian crawling around with them in the middle of a firefight, would say "Do you have to be here?" "No," I answered. "If I didn't have to I wouldn't even be here," they would say, shaking their heads and laughing at their visitor's craziness.

The relationship between soldiers and photographers has been good from the earliest days of combat photography. In Vietnam, certainly, I almost always felt welcome, particularly among the grunts. My presence connected them to home, and gave them a sense that people "back in the world" cared about what they were doing. They also appreciated the fact that I and the other shooters shared the danger with them; even when we left, they knew it was usually for another operation.

Many GIs who returned will tell you that getting out of 'Nam alive was only half the battle. Surviving mentally was the other half. We all left a bit of ourselves out there, but some left more than others. I know too many photographers who made it home safely but have never been able to get over the experience. Like Willie Vicoy, they are haunted by the memories, the good as well as the bad. Many turned to drugs and alcohol, and can't wait to run into someone from "the good old days" in order to re-live familiar war stories. For them, time stopped in Southeast Asia. For lucky others, it didn't.

The majority of good photographers who came back from Vietnam went on to bigger and better careers. Certainly photographing a war is a major milestone, but the talented ones don't need combat to make a good photograph. Drama, action, and human emotion are part of the battlefield, but not everyone with a camera is going to be able to show it. Having edited thousands of pictures taken by camera users, I can attest to that.

Everything can be taught except how to see or feel. A photographer's vision is connected directly to his or her heart. The pictures we take are an extension of both. We humans are not, by nature, objective. We see things through different eyes, therefore differently. I've always believed in objectivity as a concept and as a journalistic precept, but even though your finger pushes the shutter, your eye and your gut dictate what you take.

Most of the good shots I took in Vietnam were on the periphery of battles, not in the middle of them. I think my strongest pictures reflected the suffering, the desperation, the loneliness, and the toll war takes on the innocent people caught up in it. I've never considered myself to be particularly courageous, or to have engaged in spectacular acts of bravery. I was in Vietnam to do my job, as a professional news photographer, not as a "war photographer." War is by definition news. Risky news. More than thirty-six photographers were killed in Vietnam alone.

Every photographer dreams of capturing that one great shot, that magical moment of passage from life into death. Capa got it, with "The Falling Soldier," the Spanish civil war fighter with his arms flung out, crossing into death as the shutter is pressed. Immortality for the subject, and for the photographer. For isn't death a part of life? How many pictures are there like that one? Even Capa's icon of war photography is suspect. But there's nothing suspicious about the idea of that shot. For all the millions of pictures taken in war, the moment of death is the rarest of images. I know of only a couple that come close. Eddie Adams' picture of General Loan shooting a Viet Cong suspect in the head is one of them. Nothing questionable about that photo.

Adams' photograph underscores another point. Vietnam was not a TV war, it was a still photographer's war. Which images most affected the American public and helped form their opinion of Vietnam? Still pictures. Adams' photo, Saigon in the 1968 Tet Offensive, the My Lai massacre, Nick Ut's powerful shot of the little girl running down the road after being napalmed, and on and on. TV may have brought Vietnam into your living room, but the still pictures took it directly to your soul. Our shared memories of Vietnam, and of other wars, generally consist of a grim series of stark, still images. They are burned into our minds.

The book you're about to read contains a lot of those images. Whether they date from the Civil War or from the Gulf War, you'll find that they still have the same stark power that they did when they were first taken. But Norm Moyes' book is more than a collection of pictures. It's a testament and a tribute to all the photographers who've shared the terror and excitement of heading into battle armed only with cameras, especially to those who didn't come back.

The one story that gave me nightmares was not related to war or combat. It was Jonestown. My previous experience with the carnage of war didn't prepare me for the sight of 938 people dead in Guyana—one of the biggest mass murder/suicides in history. As I walked through that hell on earth I thought that war seemed almost civilized compared to it. But as always I raised my camera to my eye, focused, and shot. That's what I do. I'm a photographer.

—David Hume Kennerly

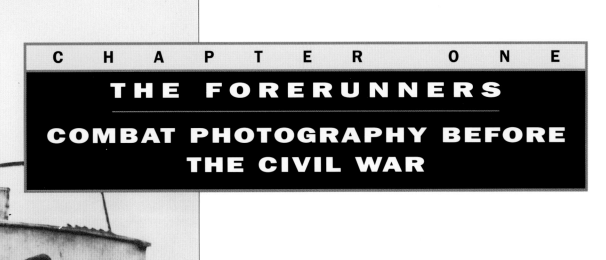

"I could have done so much more with photography in World War II if I had had today's equipment."

George Silk *of* Life *magazine*

The first pictorial documentarians of war were artists and illustrators. They seldom witnessed the scenes that they depicted, preferring to work far out of range of muskets and cannons. Mainly, they recorded victories and glorified generals, which in most cases is what they were paid to do. Their work is seriously flawed by a failure to portray the grim side of battle. On the whole, it was not a distinguished beginning.

But with the advent of photography, combat soon lost much of its glamour. The essential horror of war could not be hidden forever from the camera's discerning eye. The earliest known war photographs are five daguerreotypes by an unknown photographer, possibly from Saltillo, Mexico. One picture may be the first ever taken of a battlefield, that of Buena Vista, taken during the Mexican War (1846–48). However, Roger Fenton, founder of the Photographic Society of London, is generally regarded as the first of the war photographers. Fenton was sent by the English government in 1855 to photograph the battlefields of the Crimean War. He traveled in a closed wagon, which also served as a primitive darkroom. The Crimean heat made his work almost unendurable, often forcing him to quit by 10 A.M. "As soon as my van door was closed," he wrote, "perspiration started from every pore." Dust and flies aggravated the job of coating the wet plates, and colonels and captains pestered him for portraits.

OPPOSITE: This photo, believed to be the earliest depicting an American war scene, shows General Wool and his men posing in a Mexican town during the Mexican War (1846–48.) This picture was taken by an unknown daguerrotypist, probably sometime during 1848.

LEFT: The first time a photographer was dispatched to photograph troops in combat areas was during the Crimean War (1853–55). Roger Fenton used this wagon as a darkroom after he took what were essentially public relations pictures of British troops in the Crimea.

Fenton's cameras required long exposure times, making instantaneous shots impossible. But he would watch for quiet moments in the fighting or he would pose groups of soldiers so as to give the impression of candid action.

But Fenton, too, avoided the gruesome aspects of battle, and today his 350 photographs seem intended to reassure the public that their soldiers were well cared for.

In America, the importance of photography for military purposes was vigorously discussed in New York on June 10, 1861, at the regular meeting of the American Photographical Society.

The president of the society, John W. Draper, named a committee to approach the War Department, recommending that it consider using photography to document military action. But three months later, even though the society offered the government its services, Draper was forced to report to the group: "Little progress has been made in the matter owing to the extraordinary preoccupation of the Department."

Elsewhere, however, military leaders were beginning to acknowledge the importance of photography. The first military photographic school was founded in 1856 in Chatham, England. In 1860 the French minister of war ordered that one officer in each army corps study photography. Photographic courses were introduced at the Military Cartographic Institute in Vienna in 1862 and at the Military School in Paris in 1871.

CHAPTER TWO

THE CIVIL WAR

BRADY AND HIS BUNCH

"If any man deserves credit for accumulating materials for history, that man is M. B. Brady."

Harper's Weekly, November 14, 1863

The Civil War produced thousands of photographs, most of them taken by hometown photographers who made one or two exposures of a local battlefield and called it quits. One man, however, gained enduring fame by compiling a photographic record of each major battle: Mathew B. Brady, the father of American photojournalism.

MATHEW B. BRADY

From his boyhood, Brady was fascinated by photography. With the help of an acquaintance, the inventor Samuel F. B. Morse (who had just returned from a visit to Europe, where he had met Jacques Daguerre), Brady mastered the new art of daguerreotype. He quickly adopted new techniques, and he was a perfectionist in his work.

Before the war, Brady had become a highly successful photographer in New York City, where he was known as "Brady of Broadway." He also ran a popular gallery in Washington. He specialized in portraits of public figures, who flocked to him. A dapper man, Brady wore silk scarves, muslin shirts, linen handkerchiefs, a tailored merino vest, black doeskin pants, and a black diagonal coat. Because of his poor eyesight, he wore thick spectacles.

OPPOSITE: The large format cameras and long exposures used by Civil War photographers resulted in excellent detail and surprising sharpness. This photo, taken at City Point, Virginia in 1864 by one of the Brady photographers, shows shells and guns ready to be sent to Union troops under Ulysses S. Grant to supply his campaign in the South.

LEFT: A Union soldier takes a close look at an 11"×14" camera being used by one of Brady's photographers. The National Archives houses many of the 8"×10" and 11"×14" plates that Brady's photographers developed.

At the time of Abraham Lincoln's presidential inau-
guration, war was in the air, and Brady made preparations
to photograph the conflict. He felt certain the public
would clamor for an album of war pictures. In order to be
sure he could get to the battlefields, he went to see the
lanky new president, from whom he secured a terse, pen-
cil-written note that said, "Pass Brady."

Brady had met Lincoln during the presidential campaign, and had taken the candidate's picture in his Broadway studio. According to James Horan, in *Mathew Brady*,

Brady put Lincoln before the camera, but
somehow he had trouble getting a natural picture. Finally he asked Lincoln if he would
arrange his shirt and coat-collar. "Ah, I see you
want to shorten my neck," he said. "That's just
it, Mr. Lincoln," Brady replied. The little joke
seemed to relax Lincoln. He stared into the lens.
At the magic second, the shutter winked and the
calm, beautiful face of the great man was captured on the wet plate.

Lincoln then left the studio to deliver a well-
received speech at Cooper Institute. The newspapers
used Brady's portrait for their wood engravings, and
Currier and Ives later made striking lithographs from it.
A few years later, when Brady was visiting the White
House, Marshal Ward Hill Lamon presented him to the
president, saying, "I have not introduced Mr. Brady."
Lincoln replied, "Brady and the Cooper Institute made
me president."

Lincoln approved of Brady's plans to photograph any
conflict, but he told Brady that he must pay for the project himself, without any government help.

So on July 20, 1861, about 9 A.M., when the genteel
crowds from Washington drew up their carriages on the
hill at Centerville, Virginia, overlooking Bull Run, like
spectators getting ready to watch an athletic contest,
Brady was there, his cameras ready.

As the First Battle of Bull Run wore on, most of the
crowd was disappointed. All they could see on the wood-
ed plain below was an occasional banner, a puff of smoke,
or a glint of sunshine on a flashing saber. But later in the
day, the spectators were treated to more excitement than
they had bargained for when they were engulfed by
swarms of blue-clad soldiers in retreat. Brady kept working, ignoring the danger and confusion, even though his
wagon was overturned. He managed to save some of his
wet plates, and three days later he straggled into
Washington, greeted his wife, and rushed the plates to a
publisher.

Brady's work at Bull Run won high praise from the
press, which hailed his photographs as "the best record of

the battle" and "a spoiler of propaganda." One journal wrote that Brady showed more pluck than many of the officers and soldiers. Brady, determined to follow the entire course of the war, said, "Like Euphorion, I felt I had to go. A spirit in my feet said, 'Go' and I went."

As the war spread, Brady realized he personally would be able to record only a small fraction of the battles. So he hired about twenty skilled photographers, assigned them to various battle units, and paid for all their supplies and equipment—an expense he later estimated at $100,000. They took the pictures, but Brady took the credit, which explains why so many Civil War photos bear his name. Ironically, Brady himself took relatively few photographs of combat areas. The Library of Congress officially credits him with only fifteen.

But Lieutenant J.A. Gardner, who recalled watching Brady in action at Petersburg, Virginia, praised Brady's cool head under fire:

On June 21, 1864, Brady, the photographer, drove his light wagon out to the entrenchments. Approaching Captain Cooper, Brady politely asked if he could take a picture of the battery when just about to fire. The enemy, observing the movement of the preparations, began firing. Brady, seeing his camera was uninjured, recalled his assistant and took more pictures from a little to the rear.

After the war, Brady was beset with financial troubles. His war album did not sell, his studio business fell off, and he was faced with numerous lawsuits for nonpayment of bills and wages. Finally, in January 1873, he was forced into bankruptcy. He barely managed to pay off his debts two years later, when the government bought his Civil War collection of 5,712 plates for $25,000. He had asked for $125,000.

Destroyed Confederate cannon are scattered, while, in the background, Richmond, Virginia, lies in ruins. Note the intact Capitol building.

During the next fifteen years, Brady worked at various galleries in Washington. Until the day he died in a New York City charity hospital—January 16, 1896—he was confident that the government would publish his pictures as soon as the photoengraving process was sufficiently refined for high-quality reproduction. He also believed that his photographs would one day be highly esteemed by historians as firsthand records of the war.

His wish was fulfilled in 1911, when the Review of Reviews Company published a ten-volume work entitled *The Photographic History of the Civil War*, which included his photographs. A far superior version of Brady's work appeared in 1961 when Macmillan Company published *Divided We Fought*.

More than three hundred photographers took pictures of at least some aspect of the Civil War. Four Northern photographers—in addition to Brady—deserve special mention: Alexander Gardner, George N. Barnard, Timothy H. O'Sullivan, and John F. Gibson—all one-time employees of Mathew B. Brady. In fact, this was the quartet that made Brady famous, though all four left him in 1863.

ALEXANDER GARDNER

Alexander Gardner had been a reporter for Glasgow (Scotland) *Sentinel* and became an editor there at age twenty-eight. A socialist utopian in the style of Robert Owen, Gardner came to the United States in 1849 to set up his version of the ideal community. But the little community Gardner founded in Iowa was ravaged by tuberculosis. Gardner did his best for the survivors, then moved his family to New York City, where he got a job with Brady.

Brady took Gardner to Washington in 1858 to help run his new gallery there. When war broke out, scenes of battle were so popular and so frequently pirated that copyrighting was essential. Brady insisted that the work of any photographer in his employ was Brady's to copyright in his own name. Gardner insisted that what a photographer did on his own time with his own equipment and any profit he made belonged to the photographer alone. The two men finally split over this issue, with Gardner resigning in 1863. He set up his own gallery in Washington, patterned after Brady's, and hired his own staff for military photo copying.

BELOW: The corpses of Confederate soldiers photographed by Alexander Gardner after the Battle of Antietam.

OPPOSITE PAGE: Two of Brady's assistants are shown at Petersburg, Virginia with the wagon he used to develop his plates.

Gardner's military work was done for General George McClellan, and Gardner is given credit for three quarters of the photographs of the Army of the Potomac. He traveled a bit with the army, but usually worked in semipermanent laboratories at army headquarters. Although he rarely went into the field, several of his best-known photos are of battles and their aftermath. Some of the most famous Lincoln photographs to come out of the Civil War period were Gardner's work: Lincoln at Antietam, Lincoln's last portrait, and the hanging of Lincoln's conspirators.

In 1866, Gardner's *Photographic Sketch Book of the War*, which comprised one hundred mounted photos, became the first published collection of Civil War pictures. To his credit, Gardner meticulously listed with each photo the name of the photographer who took it.

The venture, however, was a commercial failure. Weary of war, the public had lost its appetite for scenes of ruined buildings, shattered bridges, and scarred battlefields littered with blue and gray corpses.

In 1869, four days after the nearly bankrupt Brady had petitioned Congress to buy his collection of prints, Gardner presented a similar petition. Gardner claimed that it was he, not Brady, who conceived the idea of compiling a photo history of the war, and he submitted his *Sketch Book* as evidence. The government eventually acquired his plates, but Gardner, unlike Brady, got no remuneration.

Gardner closed his Washington gallery in 1867 to travel west in the employ of the burgeoning Union Pacific Railroad. Along the Chisholm Trail, he took some of the finest pictures now extant of the frontier

life, including Indians, pioneers, covered wagons, and log cabins. He gradually lost interest in photography, however, and devoted himself to philanthropy until his death in 1882.

GEORGE N. BARNARD

George N. Barnard entered the field of photography at the age of twenty-three, only three years after Daguerre revealed his new process to the public. For more than forty years, he was in the front ranks of the rapidly developing art. When he was in his sixties, he helped the inventor George Eastman to introduce the revolutionary dry-plate process.

Before the war, Barnard was a prominent daguerreotypist in Oswego, New York, his hometown, where he took the first action news photo known to historians: a dramatic scene of the huge grain elevators that lined the river near Oswego burning to the ground on July 5, 1853. He moved to Syracuse, New York, soon after, and won widespread recognition for portraits that he entered in national contests.

Early in the war, Barnard went to the front on Brady's payroll, but in 1863 he left Brady and joined Gardner. Militarily, his most important photos were of Union and Confederate fortifications in and around Atlanta. It was Barnard who followed Major General William Tecumseh Sherman on his infamous March to the Sea. After the war, Barnard worked in Chicago—until his studio burned down—and then in Charleston, South Carolina. He died in 1902, "a kindly old man with beautiful white hair and beard."

TIMOTHY H. O'SULLIVAN

Timothy H. O'Sullivan is remembered for the most famous of Civil War pictures: "The Harvest of Death," taken at Gettysburg. O'Sullivan learned his craft in Brady's New York gallery, and he worked with Brady during the early phases of the war. But in 1863, he, too, left Brady to become Gardner's superintendent of map work. He traveled throughout Virginia, South Carolina, and Pennsylvania, taking excellent photos of many major engagements. His camera was knocked down twice by

OPPOSITE: Once-beautiful Columbia, South Carolina lies devastated after the Union bombardment. Brady photographer George Barnard is credited with taking this photo.

OPPOSITE: Ordered
by a Brady photogra-
pher to hold still for
several seconds
while he snapped
their picture, soldiers
of Benson's Battery
in the Battle of
Seven Pines, Fair
Oaks, Virginia, await
the next attack by
General Thomas
"Stonewall" Jackson.

shell fragments during bombardments, but he calmly kept taking pictures. Of the one hundred pictures in Gardner's *Sketch Book*, O'Sullivan took forty-five.

After the war, traveling with surveying teams, he photographed the West extensively. He died in 1882 at a relative's home on Staten Island.

JAMES F. GIBSON

James F. Gibson is the least known of the previously mentioned Northern photographers. A native of New York City, he, too, worked under Brady. But in 1863, like O'Sullivan and Barnard, he joined Gardner. In March 1862, while still a Brady employee, he covered the campaigns at Centerville and Bull Run. Gardner's *Sketch Book* includes thirteen of Gibson's pictures, and the Library of Congress collection has forty-eight Gibson negatives.

Many Southerners photographed the Civil War, but most of their names have been lost to history. *The Photographic History of the Civil War* offers this explanation for the shortage of records:

> The natural disappointment in the South at the end of the war was such that photographers were forced to destroy all negatives, just as owners destroyed all the objects that might serve as souvenirs or relics of the terrible struggle, thinking for the moment at least, that they could not bear the strain of brooding over the tragedy.

GEORGE S. COOK

One man won distinction, nevertheless, as the "Photographer of the Confederacy." He was George S. Cook, a native of Charleston, South Carolina. Before the war, after an unsuccessful stint in the mercantile business, Cook went to New Orleans, where he became a painter. He was attracted to daguerreotype while visiting a gallery run by some friends. He took charge of their establishment, which soon became known as one of the best galleries in the city. He joined Brady's gallery in 1851, and when Brady visited Europe in July of that year, Cook ran the studio. But when war broke out, he returned to the South.

In 1863, Cook risked his life photographing the Union fleet as it bombarded Fort Sumter. Later in the war, as the South suffered shortages of all sorts of goods, he was ingenious in procuring chemicals and other supplies from a New York company; he smuggled them into the South disguised as quinine.

A.J. LYTLE

Another Confederate photographer, A.J. Lytle, has the honor of being the first known spy-photographer. Lytle covered the war for three years while maintaining a studio on Main Street in Baton Rouge, while all the time serving as an undercover employee of the Confederate Secret Service.

He used to climb to the observation tower on Scott's Bluff to relay coded messages with a flag or a lantern to the Confederates near New Orleans. Northern sharpshooters spotted him, however, and they soon made the task so dangerous that he had to discontinue it. According to *The Photographic History of the Civil War*,

> With a courage and skill as remarkable as that of Brady himself this Confederate photographer [Lytle] risked his life to obtain negatives of Federal batteries, cavalry regiments and camps, lookout towers, and the vessels of Farragut and

Cook took the first picture of ironclads in action. The caption in *The Photographic History of the Civil War* relates the story behind the picture

On the highest point of the battered dust heap that was the still untaken fortress of Sumter, the Confederate photographer, Cook, planted his camera on September 8, 1863, and took the first photograph of ironclads in action—the monitors Weehawken, Montauk and Passaic, as they were actually firing on the Confederate batteries at Fort Moultrie. The three low-freeboarded vessels, lying almost blows-on, at the distance of nearly two miles [3.2km], look like great iron buoys in the channel, but the smoke from their heavy guns is drifting over the water, and the flames can almost be seen leaping from the turret ports. Although Fort Moultrie was the aim of their gunners, Cook, with his head under the dark cloth, saw on the ground glass a shell passing within a few feet of him. Another shell knocked one of his plate-holders off the parapet into the rain-water cistern. He gave a soldier five dollars to fish it out for him. He got his picture—and was ordered off the parapet, since he was drawing upon the fort the fire of all the Union batteries on Morris Island.

OPPOSITE: The most famous of all Civil War photos was this picture of Union dead at Gettysburg by Timothy O'Sullivan, entitled "Harvest of Death."

BELOW: This remarkable photo shows engineers and stokers on a Civil War ship.

Porter, in fact of everything that might be of the slightest use in informing the Confederate Secret Service of the strength of the Federal occupation of Baton Rouge. In Lytle's little shop on Main Street these negatives remained in oblivion for near half a century. War photographs were long regarded with extreme disfavor in the South, and the North knew nothing of Lytle's collection.

In summary, when one considers the crude state of photographic technology at the time of the Civil War, it is amazing that so many photos of that conflict compare so favorably with combat photos taken today. Even for studio photographers of the early 1860s, the processes involved in taking, developing, and printing a picture were extremely complicated and cumbersome. To duplicate these processes on the battlefield, working in horse-drawn wagons, required great skill and a lot of luck. A sudden change in humidity could ruin a plate; a spot of dust could mar it.

Unlike the dry plates that were developed later, the wet plates had surfaces that could not be touched. Getting to the scene of action with a heavy wagon, a darkroom tent, several hundred fragile glass plates, and chemicals—along back country roads that were ridged with iron-hard ruts in winter and that turned into gooey morasses in spring thaws, and in constant danger from sharpshooters, bushwhackers, and cavalry raiders—was, to say the least, an adventure. Films and lenses required long exposures, making action scenes very difficult.

Many photographers were content with pictures of the dead, the ruins, and the generals. But there were also those rare men who left a legacy of courage and ingenuity that is made richer by the physical dangers and technical obstructions that they had to overcome.

In the 1899 *Anthony's Photographic Bulletin,* Captain A.J. Russell recalled the exploits of photographer T.C. Roche during the march toward Petersburg

The enemy were bombarding the works from Howlett's Point, throwing immense shells every few minutes, tearing up the ground and raising a small earthquake every time one of them exploded. [Roche] had taken a number of views and had but one more to make to finish up the most interesting points, and this one was to be from the most exposed position. He was within a few rods of the place when down came with the whirlwind a ten-inch [25.4cm] shell, which exploded, throwing the dirt in all directions; but nothing daunted and shaking the dust from his head and camera, he quickly moved to the spot, and placing it over the pit made by the explosion, exposed his plate so coolly as if there were no danger, as if working in a country barnyard. The work finished, he quickly folded his tripod and returned to cover. I asked him if he was scared. "Scared?" he said. "Two shots never fell in the same place." At this moment the heavy boom of cannons was heard in the direction of Petersburg. Roche jumped to his feet, and rushing to the door, said, "Cap, the ball has opened; I must be off," and called to his assistant. In the next quarter of an hour two horses were harnessed, everything snugly packed, and shaking my hand with a "we will meet tomorrow at the front," said good-bye, and the wagon rattled off into the darkness of midnight towards that doomed city above which was such another display of pyrotechnics as few photos have ever witnessed—shells flying in all directions, leaving their trails of fire and fading away only to be replaced by others. ... In the morning Petersburg was ours. I found Mr. Roche on the ramparts with scores of negatives taken where the fight had been the thickest and where the harvest of death had indeed been gathered—pictures that will in truth teach coming generations that war is a terrible reality. A few minutes later I saw his van flaying towards the war-stricken city, and in the wake of the fleeing enemy. Many were the records he preserved that day that will last while history endures to relate the eventful story of a victory sorely won.

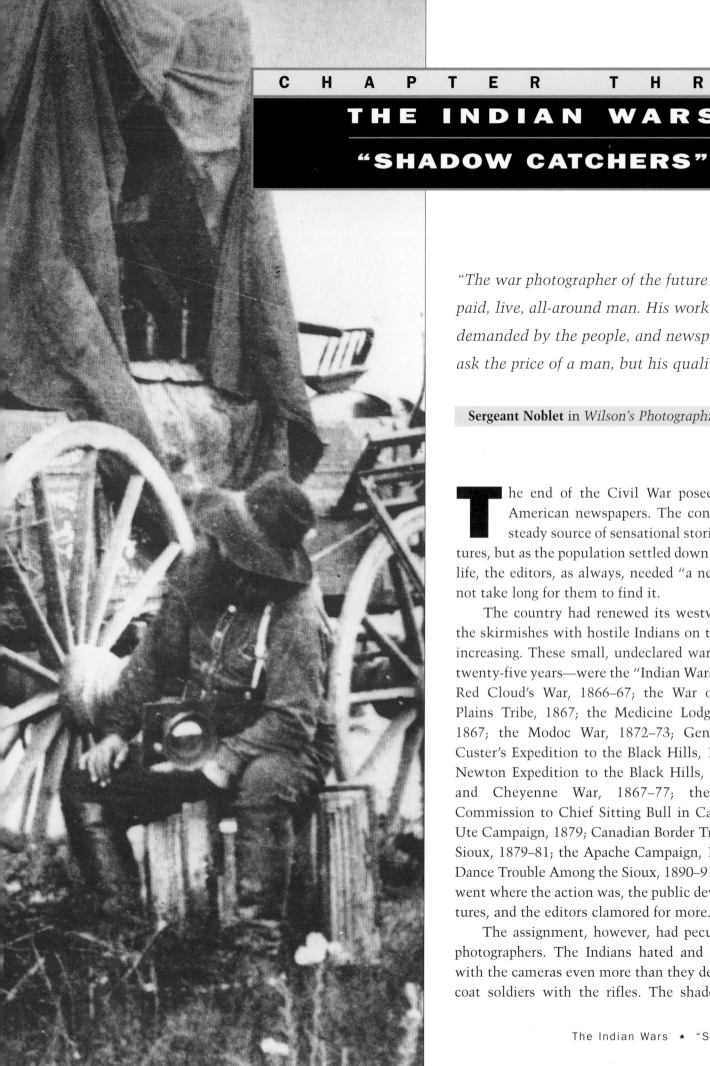

CHAPTER THREE

THE INDIAN WARS

"SHADOW CATCHERS"

"The war photographer of the future will be a well paid, live, all-around man. His work will be demanded by the people, and newspapers will not ask the price of a man, but his quality."

Sergeant Noblet in *Wilson's Photographic Journal*, 1899

The end of the Civil War posed a problem for American newspapers. The conflict had been a steady source of sensational stories and vivid pictures, but as the population settled down again to civilian life, the editors, as always, needed "a new angle." It did not take long for them to find it.

The country had renewed its westward thrust, and the skirmishes with hostile Indians on the frontier were increasing. These small, undeclared wars—which lasted twenty-five years—were the "Indian Wars." They include Red Cloud's War, 1866–67; the War of the Southern Plains Tribe, 1867; the Medicine Lodge Peace Treaty, 1867; the Modoc War, 1872–73; General George A. Custer's Expedition to the Black Hills, 1874; the Jenny-Newton Expedition to the Black Hills, 1875; the Sioux and Cheyenne War, 1867–77; the Terry Peace Commission to Chief Sitting Bull in Canada, 1877; the Ute Campaign, 1879; Canadian Border Troubles with the Sioux, 1879–81; the Apache Campaign, 1881; and Ghost Dance Trouble Among the Sioux, 1890–91. Photographers went where the action was, the public devoured their pictures, and the editors clamored for more.

The assignment, however, had peculiar hazards for photographers. The Indians hated and feared the men with the cameras even more than they despised the blue-coat soldiers with the rifles. The shadowy, black-and-

OPPOSITE: U.S. Army soldiers crouch behind boulders as they fight rebellious Indians during the Modoc campaign of the Indian Wars of 1872–73. This photo, from the U.S. Army, may have been taken by Eadweard Muybridge.

LEFT: Alexander Gardner, who took some of the greatest Civil War photos, went west after the war to photograph frontier life in Kansas and Oklahoma as well as the Indian Wars. Here he's shown seated with his camera lens on his lap.

white quality of the photographs alarmed the Indians. The Cheyenne believed that a photographic print actually was a man's shadow. They feared that if the picture were taken away, the man's spirit would be taken away, too, and the man would die. The Plains Indians cursed photographers as "shadow catchers."

RIDGEWAY GLOVER

Ridgeway Glover, a young Philadelphia photographer, was one of the first to try to take pictures of hostilities with Indians. In early July 1866, as a special artist correspondent for *Leslie's Illustrated Newspaper*, Glover got on an army train headed from Fort Laramie to Fort Kearney. His assignment: to illustrate the life and character of the wild men of the prairie.

The train, escorted by five officers and a detachment of the Eighteenth Infantry, was attacked by Sioux Indians near Crazy Woman's Fork of the Powder River. Glover described the attack in a letter to his paper a week later:

Our men with their rifles held the Indians at bay until we reached a better position on a hill, where we kept them off until night when Captain Burroughs, coming up with a train, caused the red-skins to retreat. I desired to make some instantaneous views of the Indian attack but our commander ordered me not to.

David White, the post chaplain, survived the attack, and said that Glover "behaved with great coolness and bravery for a noncombatant."

A month after the incident, Glover was still at Fort Kearney waiting for some chemicals to arrive from the East on a medical supply train. He was reckless with his personal safety during this interval, often traveling alone to the snow range of the Bighorn Mountains armed with nothing but a butcher knife.

Soon after the chemicals reached the fort in September, Glover and a friend set out to take some pictures. Their bodies were found six miles [4.6 km] away, scalped and mutilated, presumably by Arapaho Indians. Glover's total output during his brief career in the West amounted to twenty-one successful prints.

WILLIAM H. JACKSON

Perhaps the best frontier photographer was William H. Jackson. Jackson became a professional photographer in Omaha in 1868, when he was twenty-five. He joined a government-sponsored survey of the West in 1869, working for ten years as the group's official photographer. While traveling the Oregon Trail, he persuaded Washakie, a Shoshone chief, to let Jackson photograph him and his tribe. The pictures are among the few extant today showing Indians in their native habitat. In 1872, Jackson's photographs of Yellowstone country helped persuade Congress to declare the area a national park.

CHARLES R. SAVAGE

English-born Charles R. Savage, who became a Mormon and migrated to Utah, was another outstanding photographer of the West. His most famous pictures were taken on May 10, 1869, at Promontory Point, Utah, and

Gathering up the Dead at the Battle Field at Wounded Knee

show the golden spike being driven to mark the completion of the railroad that spanned the country. To any photographer with a notion to come West, Savage had this advice: "You must have plenty of time at your disposal, a strong party well armed with Henry rifles, and good animals."

General Custer's foray into the Black Hills of the Dakotas was photographed by W.H. Illingworth of St. Paul, Minnesota. But Illingworth managed to be elsewhere during the incident that secured the general's dubious place in American history. Illingworth's editors, no doubt, had mixed feelings about his good fortune. Another photographer, S.J. Morrow, went to the battlefield at Little Bighorn a year later and took some excellent photos of the terrain.

One picture to come out of the Indian War period has a particularly colorful history. The photo was taken in January 1891 by frontier photographer J.C.H. Grabill of Deadwood, South Dakota. The picture shows eleven correspondents who were covering the Sioux Ghost Dance Rebellion, and it happened to include Colonel. W.F.

"Buffalo Bill" Cody. As Grabill took the picture, Alfred I. Burkholder, a correspondent with the New York *Herald*, moved his head, blurring his face in the print. As a result, Grabill refused to give out any prints. Two years later, another *Herald* writer, Edgar F. Medary, tried to buy a print. The fussy photographer agreed, but only on the condition that Medary promise not to reproduce the print until after Grabill's death.

In October 1921, Medary took the print with him to Honolulu for the Press Congress of the World. An alert reporter for the Honolulu *Advertiser*, seeing a good feature, asked permission to reproduce the photo of the reporters and Cody in his paper.

Medary agreed, knowing that Grabill had died some years before. The picture of Buffalo Bill finally appeared, thirty years later and thousands of miles from the place where it was taken.

Fortunately for historians, Indian War photographers picked up where the Civil War photographers had left off. Their photos document an exciting and important episode in the history of American expansion.

Wearing their ceremonial regalia, these Sioux Indians, with Chief Big Foot, pose for photographer J.C.H. Grabill at the Standing Rock Agency during the summer of 1890.

THE SPANISH–AMERICAN WAR
OUR MEN IN HAVANA

"I consider myself fortunate in being one of the few photographers who have had the privilege and opportunity to reproduce the stirring and splendid pictures of this exciting time. I found that while I was exposed to the dangers of the bullets and the breaking of shells around me, my work kept me preoccupied; that I really forgot in a great many instances that I was on the field of battle."

John C. Hemment, 1899

The Spanish-American War lasted only four months, from June to September, 1898. It was primarily a naval war; the army conducted only three campaigns, and the only serious fighting was in the Santiago campaign. Fewer than two hundred Americans were killed in action, although many more died from other war-related causes.

In spite of its brevity, the Spanish-American War produced two outstanding combat photographers: John C. Hemment of the New York *Journal* and James H. Hare of *Collier's*.

JOHN C. HEMMENT

Born in New York City in about 1873, John Hemment opened a studio in Brooklyn in his early twenties. He was then sent to Havana by the United States Government to take photos of the battleship *Maine*, which had been ripped by an explosion.

Instead of coming back to the United States when the assignment was finished, he lingered in Havana to

OPPOSITE: Intrepid New York *Journal* photographer John C. Hemment photographed Spanish-American War troops assembling in a valley near San Juan Hill.
LEFT: A U.S. Army photographer holds the tripod to his 5"×7" camera as he rides in a boat following the advance of troops near Candaba in the Phillipines in April 1899.

photograph Spanish fortifications. He was caught in the act, but before the police arrested him as a spy, Hemment managed to slip his photographic plates to a sympathetic Cuban, instructing him not to let the Spaniards get them. He then avoided trial by bribing a guard to let him go, and after retrieving his plates, he escaped from Cuba by bribing a customs agent to get him onto a ship bound for New York.

When hostilities broke out, he returned to Cuba on a ship owned and captained by his boss, William Randolph Hearst. Hemment, an audacious photographer, floated aloft at Santiago in a balloon to take pictures of Spanish trenches and batteries. When the Spanish fleet was destroyed, he helped capture a few docile Spanish sailors who were fleeing their sinking ships. His pictures—all of which bear the copyright "W.R. Hearst"—include the wreckage of the *Maine*, fortifications at Havana Harbor, the Rough Riders, Morro Castle, aerial photos of Spanish trenches, and American warships.

To get good prints, he fought a constant battle with the heat and humidity. He finally found that the best place to work, when possible, was on the shady side of a ship's deck with large quantities of ice nearby.

Hemment returned to New York on the same ship with Teddy Roosevelt's Rough Riders. Once home, he continued to work for the *Journal*. He was the only American photographer to cover China's Boxer Rebellion in 1901. Later, while on assignment with an exploring expedition to Africa, he was bitten by a tsetse fly and contracted sleeping sickness. He died in England in 1927.

OPPOSITE: Elements of Colonel Theodore Roosevelt's Rough Riders following the ride up San Juan Hill in 1898.

BELOW: A detachment of 1.65-inch guns of the Sixth Light Artillery take up positions in 1899 in the Phillipines.

OPPOSITE: William
Dinwiddie photo-
graphed members
of the Sixteenth
Infantry Regiment as
they are being fired
on during the battle
of San Juan Hill on
July 1, 1898.

The *Journal* praised him as "probably the best out-door and instantaneous photographer in the country." Writer and soldier W.I. Lincoln called him "the first photographer to obtain a complete pictorial description of an entire war."

> ## Shortly after the war, Hemment, in *Cannon and Camera*, offered some advice to future combat photographers
>
> While it is necessary to have good lenses, good cameras, good plates, and, in fact, everything good in the line of tools, ...there must be something more than this. The camera is like the gun of the war ship; while the gun can do the deadly execution, ...the man must be behind the gun. So it is with the camera.
>
> To the professional photographer who goes to the front, ...I would give the advice to use as small a camera as possible to render the picture properly discernible. ...I would advise the use of a rapid-working lens, no matter whose make it may be, as long as it has that ...property of dealing with a large, plain field, good depth of focus, and plenty of brilliancy...It has been said of the gallant men who fight on the line that they forget the danger when they once commence their work, and I positively believe such is the case. It is one's duty to depict that which seems to be the best. While I cannot say that I long to see another war, ...should a chance present itself in the future for me to do what I have done in the past, I think I could do myself, and the profession in general, more credit than I have hitherto.

JAMES H. HARE

A man who accompanied James H. Hare on many combat assignments noted, "No war is official until covered by Jimmy Hare." Hare deserved the accolade, for besides covering the Spanish-American War, he also pho-

Several years after it was destroyed in February 1898, the shattered hulk of the battleship _Maine_ was partially raised in Havana Harbor, when this picture was taken. The ship was towed to a point off the Cuban coast and sunk.

tographed the Russian-Japanese War, the Mexican Insurrection, and World War I.

Born in London in 1856, the son of a prominent manufacturer of expensive cameras, Hare began taking pictures while still a boy. He moved to the United States in 1889, settled in Brooklyn, and worked for various New York publications. Just before the war broke out, a fire destroyed the _Illustrated American_, where he worked, wiping out most of his equipment and leaving him without a job.

When the _Maine_ sank in Havana Harbor, Hare saw his chance. He dashed to the Manhattan offices of Robert J. Collier, editor of _Collier's Weekly_, and offered to go to Cuba for five dollars a day to get exclusive photographs.

Collier, who promptly hired him, later recalled, "The _Maine_ blew up and Jimmy blew in. Both were major explosions."

When Hare got to Havana, he took pictures of the _Maine_ wreckage, rebel prisoners, the American consul general, and human interest shots of the _Maine_'s chaplain comforting the wounded and identifying the dead. The photographs caused a sensation in _Collier's_ offices when they reached New York, and Hare was given an immediate raise in salary.

After taking the pictures, however, Hare had no way to get back to the United States. He ran into a newspaperman who said that he had a ship waiting about 20 miles [32 km] from Havana, and the two men set off for

the rendezvous. But they got lost in the jungle for six days, and the ship had already left when they reached the designated spot. Fortunately, they spotted an American gunboat on the horizon, and they forced some Cuban fishermen to row them to the ship.

When hostilities broke out, Hare returned to Cuba at once. He risked death repeatedly to get photographs of troops on the front lines. Once, while photographing soldiers near San Juan Hill, an enemy shell exploded only a few feet away, killing two men near him.

Like all photographers of the Spanish-American War, Hare was at first hampered in his work by the sticky, tropical climate, which made his negatives melt slightly. But he learned a trick from a Cuban of spraying the neg-

atives with alcohol, offsetting the heat with cooling evaporation. He was often complimented by *Collier's* for his consistently sharp pictures, while other magazines had to use fuzzy prints.

FRANCES BENJAMIN JOHNSTON

The Spanish-American War also gave us the first American woman photographer to cover combat areas: Frances Benjamin Johnston, a young woman who arrived in Cuba near the end of the war. She made up for her late start, however, by taking outstanding pictures aboard the USS *Olympia*, Admiral Dewey's flagship.

Signal Corps Sergeant Harry W. Chadwick photographed the Kansas Volunteer Infantry on March 7, 1899 as they fired on Philippine Insurrectionists.

Born in 1864 in West Virginia, Johnston studied art in Paris, then worked as a newspaper columnist in Washington. She took up professional photography in 1888, the year the war broke out, and she quickly distinguished herself as a news and feature photographer—the first American woman to do so.

WILLIAM DINWIDDIE

A nod of recognition must be given to another photographer of the Spanish-American War, William Dinwiddie. Dinwiddie won a small niche in history by snapping the best-known photo of the war—the charge of Teddy Roosevelt and his Rough Riders up San Juan Hill.

This war was the first to be covered by U.S. Army Signal Corps photographers. These men were trained at Fort Riley, Kansas, some of them by Mathew Brady himself. They worked on a small scale, however, because the Signal Corps was not officially given the photographic mission of the army until many years later. The Corps increased its activity during the Philippine Insurrection (1898–1913), which consisted of about a dozen skirmishes between Americans and a small band of Filipinos.

Tremendous advances in photographic technology were being made during this period. A dozen years before the war, George Eastman developed the perfect amateur camera of its day—a small box he called a "Kodak." Anyone could use it. The directions read: 1) Point the camera, 2) Press the button, 3) Turn the key, and 4) Pull the cord. Each roll of film had one hundred negatives.

When the roll was fully exposed, the entire camera was mailed to Eastman's factory in Rochester, New York, where it was reloaded and returned with the negatives and one hundred mounted prints, all for a cost of ten dollars. The original cost for the first loaded camera was twenty-five dollars.

The new hobby was an instant success. Eastman was well on his way to making his first million when United States troops were sent to Cuba, many of them carrying his new invention with them. When the war ended, the War Department, thinking that some of the photos might have historical significance, asked the men to send in their war photographs. Thousands of snapshots were submitted, but the results were disappointing. The enlargements were finally placed in two unpublished albums

OPPOSITE: Colonel Theodore "Teddy" Roosevelt strikes a pose for James Hare of *Collier's* Magazine as he prepares to lead his Rough Riders up San Juan Hill.

OPPOSITE: The first woman to take pictures in combat areas, Frances Benjamin Johnston photographed many naval scenes during the Spanish-American War. This photo, taken in 1898, shows the USS *Maine*.

BELOW: A donkey pulls a railroad cart carrying a group of Signal Corps photographers from San Fernando to Manila on May 15, 1899.

entitled "Scenes and Incidents Connected with the War between the United States and Spain."

Meanwhile, the U.S. Army Signal Corps was slowly taking over the task of documenting wars for posterity. America's first military photographer, Sergeant George W. Rice, was sent by the Signal Corps on the ill-fated Arctic expedition of 1881; he was one of the men on the trip who starved to death in 1884. At that time, a school to train noncommissioned officers in photography was established at Fort Riley, Kansas. A Signal Corps photographic training manual suggested in 1896 that a photographic section be assigned to each divisional headquarters.

During the assault on Manila in August 1898, Sergeant Harry W. Chadwick took the Signal Corps' first official photographs of the United States Army in combat. The first Signal Corps photographer captured by the enemy was Sergeant J.D. Saulsbury, who was held prisoner for about six months in 1899 by the Philippine Insurrectionists.

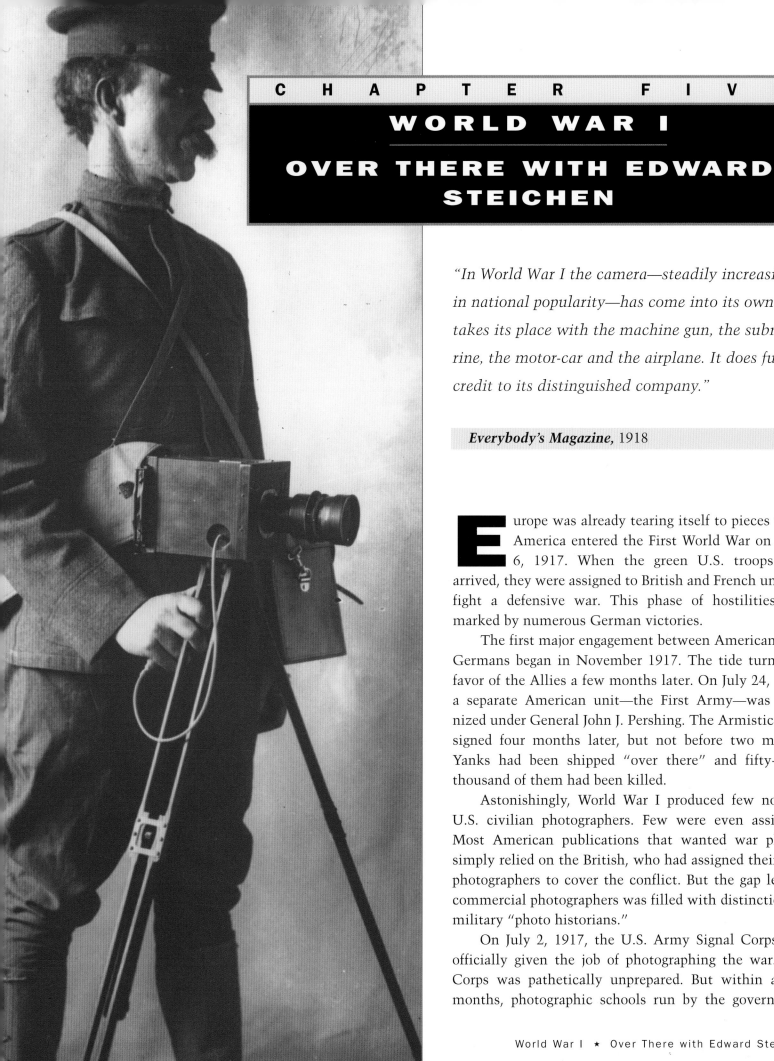

WORLD WAR I

OVER THERE WITH EDWARD STEICHEN

"In World War I the camera—steadily increasing in national popularity—has come into its own. It takes its place with the machine gun, the submarine, the motor-car and the airplane. It does full credit to its distinguished company."

Everybody's Magazine, 1918

Europe was already tearing itself to pieces when America entered the First World War on April 6, 1917. When the green U.S. troops first arrived, they were assigned to British and French units to fight a defensive war. This phase of hostilities was marked by numerous German victories.

The first major engagement between Americans and Germans began in November 1917. The tide turned in favor of the Allies a few months later. On July 24, 1918, a separate American unit—the First Army—was organized under General John J. Pershing. The Armistice was signed four months later, but not before two million Yanks had been shipped "over there" and fifty-three thousand of them had been killed.

Astonishingly, World War I produced few notable U.S. civilian photographers. Few were even assigned. Most American publications that wanted war photos simply relied on the British, who had assigned their best photographers to cover the conflict. But the gap left by commercial photographers was filled with distinction by military "photo historians."

On July 2, 1917, the U.S. Army Signal Corps was officially given the job of photographing the war. The Corps was pathetically unprepared. But within a few months, photographic schools run by the government

OPPOSITE: This photo, released by the "Committee on Public Information" on January 31, 1918, shows two Doughboys helping a wounded comrade to a hospital behind the front lines in France.
LEFT: A Signal Corps sergeant poses with a camera equipped with a telephoto lens and tripod. Cameras similar to this were used by Army photographers during World War I.

OPPOSITE: This, the most famous photo of World War I, was taken by an unknown Signal Corps photographer during fighting on the Western Front. Soldiers of the Twenty-third Infantry Regiment of the Second Division fire a 37mm gun at a German position in France.

were training and equipping hundreds, then thousands, of combat photographers.

Before the war was over, thirty-eight fully equipped divisional photographic units were shipped overseas, comprising fifty-four officers and 418 men, plus one unit that was sent to Siberia. These men took hundreds of thousands of pictures. In almost any single day of the Meus-Argonne offensive, for example, more pictures were taken by military photographers than were made during the entire Civil War by civilian and military photographers of the Union and the Confederacy combined.

However, the failure of many officers to appreciate the value of photographic records often resulted in a lack of transportation for photographers and their equipment. It was hard to get photographic supplies to France even after they had been paid for because priority was given to food and munitions, which were often scarce. Mobile laboratory units were few and far between right up to the end of the war.

The camera had come into its own as a precision instrument by this time. Most of the photographers used a Kodak Graflex, a four-by-five inch [10.2-by-12.7cm] camera with a ten-inch [25.4cm] lens. The camera took excellent pictures, but in combat conditions it had one hazardous defect: one had to look down into it to focus it, which often meant exposing one's head to enemy fire.

EDWARD STEICHEN

The most famous photographer of World War I was Edward Steichen, a native of Milwaukee. In his teens, he had been attracted to painting, but when he reached age twenty his interests turned to photography. One of his pictures caught the eye of Alfred Stieglitz, a leading photographer of the time, and Steichen was on his way to New York to become Stieglitz's protégé. Soon Steichen won a reputation as a top photographer in his own right.

On May 7, 1915, when news reached New York that the British luxury liner *Lusitania* had been sunk by a German submarine, Steichen and Stieglitz got into a bitter argument. The German-born Stieglitz said, "It served [the British] right. They were warned in advance that the ship would be sunk." Steichen, who had visited Paris and had taken a famous photo of Rodin, regarded France, which was Britain's ally, as a second mother country.

Edward Steichen,
who photographed
both world wars,
poses with members
of his photographic
section in France.

Steichen said, "I decided then and there that I wanted to get into the war on the American [Allied] side. I wanted to be a photographic reporter as Mathew Brady had been in the Civil War, and I went to Washington to offer my services."

He enlisted in the Signal Corps and soon took up aerial photography. He reached his beloved France with the first small contingent of American troops in June 1917 and was immediately put in charge of training aerial photographers.

> **Steichen was a sensitive man who was deeply troubled by the moral contradictions of war and by his part in it. He later recalled his thoughts on the night of November 11, 1918, when after a bitter day of carnage he went to his barracks and lay down on the bed.**

The whole monstrous horror of the war seemed to fall down on me and smother me. I smelled the rotting carcasses of dead horses, saw the three white faces of the first American dead that I had seen. I could hear the rat-a-tat-tat of the machine-gun fire as one lay flat on one's belly trying to dig into the earth to escape it, and the ping-ping-ping of the bullets coming through the leaves overhead. I saw the dried blood around the bullet hole in a young soldier's head. And he was only one of hundreds of thousands. How could men and nations have been so stupid? What was the use of living?

I had never had to come face-to-face with another man and shoot him and see him crumple up and fall, yet I could not deny to myself having played a role in the slaughter. I had never been conscious of anything but the job we had to do: photograph enemy territory and enemy actions, record enemy movements and gun emplacements, pinpoint the targets for our own artillery. The work had been full of organizational difficulties. We had had to improvise all along the way with inadequate equipment and materials and inadequately trained personnel. But the photographs we made provided information that, conveyed to our artillery, enabled them to destroy their targets and kill.

From Newhall, *Masters of Photography*

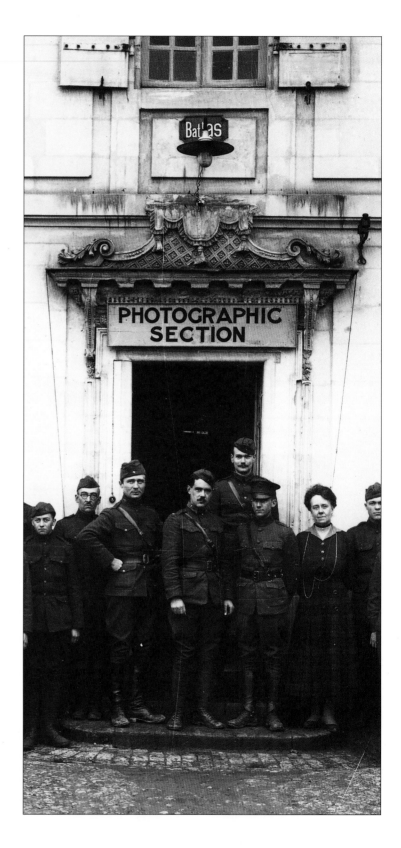

A year later, during the Second Battle of the Marne, Steichen met the famous General Billy Mitchell. "The first question he asked me after the formal introduction," Steichen recalled, "was, 'when are we going to get any 90-centimeter cameras for the high altitude photography?' "

"Sir," Steichen replied, "we have six already."

"Well," Mitchell demanded, "why aren't they in use?" Steichen explained that the pilots in the observation squadrons objected to the cameras because they took up so much room that the gunner could not work his weapon.

Mitchell said, "Well, can you get one out here? I'll take it up."

Steichen had a camera delivered from the supply depot in Paris the same day. "After asking me several questions about aerial photography processing," Steichen recalled, "General Mitchell seemed convinced that I knew what I was talking about and that I understood the urgent need for equipment and materials. He put in an order for me to be attached to his service during each important military operation."

Steichen's work at the front won him several promotions, and by the end of the war he was a full colonel. After the war, he returned to the United States. Steichen turned his talents to industrial advertising and high fashion and became the best advertising photographer of his day.

It was during World War I that aerial photography became a significant factor in strategic planning. At the time war was declared, the new science was almost unknown in the United States.

Napoleon III was the first military leader to make good use of aerial photography, when in 1859, during the battle of Solferino, he had the Austrian positions photographed. By 1880, sharp, instantaneous pictures could be taken from balloons.

In March 1917, the Air Service developed an aerial "gun camera" equipped with a trigger and Springfield rifle sights. It was fitted with a 24-inch [61cm] telephoto lens that could photograph a full square mile [2.6km] of topography from two miles [3.2km] up. The new lens let reconnaissance pilots fly at altitudes of 12,000 feet [3,600m], far out of range of German antiaircraft fire, which at the end of the war was deadly accurate. Because the weight of the photo equipment made the camera planes slow, they had to be escorted by fighter planes. At first, the jiggling of the planes made prints turn out fuzzy.

As bombs explode in the background, wounded soldiers are given first aid treatment along the British front during a World War I engagement.

BELOW: American soldiers with fixed bayonets go over the top, following their officer into battle in France.

OPPOSITE: During a respite from the fighting in France on June 29, 1915, this Doughboy reads a letter from home.

In 1919, Signal Corps photographer Edward R. Trabold published this remarkable account of his first combat mission—the assault on Cantigny, France— in the *Photographic Journal of America.*

The captain said the boys were getting ready to go over. "Come Trabold, we will start a little war of our own."

In order to reach the spot from where our boys were going over the top it was necessary to make a slight detour, so the Huns would not see us. From time to time we halted in our rush, not only to catch our breath, but also to look through our woodland screen to see if we were going to be in time. Up to this time I had never seen anyone killed or wounded, nor had I ever taken any real front-line pictures. Sooner than I expected I got this chance.... As I rounded the side of a large tree I saw a soldier lying across a fallen tree. It looked to me as if his arm was almost off; but the captain was an old campaigner, and this was not his first war, and quickly breaking open his first-aid kit, he got busy. When he got the wound fixed up there hove in sight two stretcher-bearers who quickly took the boy to cover....

When we got to the front our boys were already on the way across, and I hastily snapped pictures. The light was against me, as the sun shone almost directly into my lens, so I had to make cross shots. Shells were bursting all around, and I secured several fine shots of them. In twenty-five minutes the boys reached Cantigny. The loss up to then was slight.

After I made a lot of pictures along the front, the captain said, "Well, old man, we will try to get to the rear and get something to eat."...

We were "balling the jack" in fine style, and the captain had just leaped a large shell-hole, and I was all ready getting myself together for a spring, when a big one lit to my right, wounding me in the hand and knocking me into the shell-hole.

The captain stopped and said, "Come on, don't waste time."

I tried to, but found that my ankle was sprained; but I got out of that hole quicker than anyone you may have seen and hobbled along.... I spotted a big dugout just then, and called the captain, and I just fell into it, landing at the bottom in a heap.

The captain said, "We will now have a look at your ankle."

Well, we found that a machine-gun bullet had gone through this, but not touched any bones, although I was sure it was all blown off. We used up the rest of our first-aid kit on this, and then decided that we would start once more to the rear.

Our course now led downhill, through barbed wire and a hillside pitted with shell holes, and also full of small brush, which made it hard going for me, but I sure did move and was close behind the captain when we reached the valley. There was a path running through this valley, and the Huns were shelling this at intervals. As we reached the bottom I noticed ahead of us a French soldier running and behind us an American officer. One shell struck near the Frenchman and another one near the American officer. Both of these men were killed. We went over to both of them, but could not render either one of them any aid, so went on to the first-aid station, where I had my wounds dressed again. About this time old Jerry got busy and began sending in gas shells near the first-aid station, and for the first time, I found use for my gas mask. They kept this up for more than an hour. I made quite a number of first-aid pictures at this spot. There were about fifteen men in front of this station who had died.

The problem was solved by the novel method of mounting the cameras on top of tennis balls, which absorbed the vibrations from the engines.

To speed the process of developing the film, which sometimes was a matter of strategic importance, the pilots often put the film or plates in a metal container and dropped it with a miniature parachute. Toward the end of the war, the Air Service was turning out an average of ten thousand prints a day.

This, then, was the First World War, photographed in detail by a rapidly growing corps of military photographers. To the military's lasting credit, it must be said that the state of the art did not suffer in their hands. To the contrary, at the end of the war, combat photography had become a highly refined craft. The chief Signal Corps officer wrote:

It is a grand stride from the methods employed by Mathew Brady, who during the Civil War made his wet plates in the field, drove through the lines of the Union army, using a camera with a lens made for spectacle glass, taking photographs which later were developed in the shelter of some barn with uncertainty as to results, to the present-day photographer conveyed to points of vantage by motorcycle, automobile, or airplane equipped with his graphic camera containing a lens from the finest of optical glass, high-speed shutter dry-plates, and cut film, which enable him to make still pictures of objects moving at high rates of speed, and with the aid of a portable darkroom produce a finished print of a still photograph in the field within fifteen minutes.

The Army had no special arrangements for civilian photographers, and they got around any way they could. In 1917, this account by Albert K. Dawson appeared in *Photo Era* magazine

[Dawson marched on foot with the infantry, rode on horseback with the cavalry, and hitched rides in automobiles with the staff officers]

It was much more interesting in this way, for I saw and got pictures of a lot of interesting things which I probably would never have been allowed to go near had I been personally conducted.... The war photographer's life is exactly like that of the soldier. He eats from the same kitchen on wheels, he travels and sleeps in the same boxcar, and the daily risks are the same for both. Naturally, after a few months of service, the camera-man gets hardened to field conditions, so that doing 25 or 30 miles [40–48km] on foot becomes just a part of the day's work, and sleeping on the ground is a matter of course.

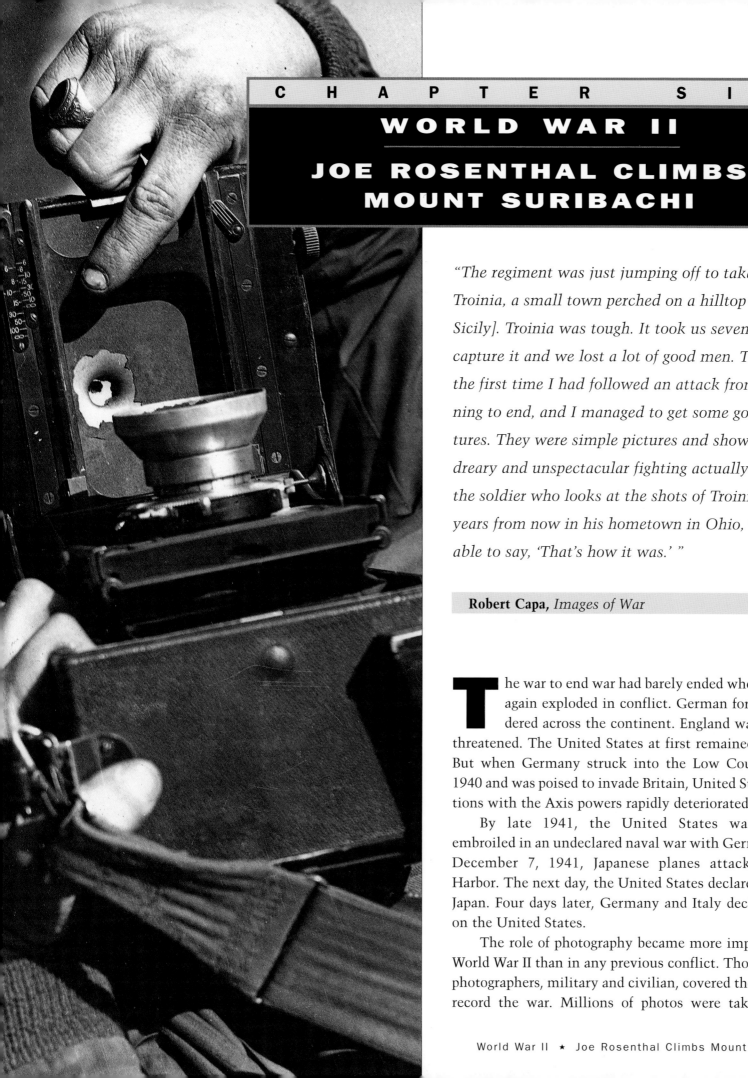

CHAPTER SIX

WORLD WAR II

JOE ROSENTHAL CLIMBS MOUNT SURIBACHI

"The regiment was just jumping off to take Troinia, a small town perched on a hilltop [in Sicily]. Troinia was tough. It took us seven days to capture it and we lost a lot of good men. This was the first time I had followed an attack from beginning to end, and I managed to get some good pictures. They were simple pictures and showed how dreary and unspectacular fighting actually is. But the soldier who looks at the shots of Troinia, ten years from now in his hometown in Ohio, will be able to say, 'That's how it was.' "

Robert Capa, *Images of War*

The war to end war had barely ended when Europe again exploded in conflict. German forces thundered across the continent. England was gravely threatened. The United States at first remained neutral. But when Germany struck into the Low Countries in 1940 and was poised to invade Britain, United States relations with the Axis powers rapidly deteriorated.

By late 1941, the United States was deeply embroiled in an undeclared naval war with Germany. On December 7, 1941, Japanese planes attacked Pearl Harbor. The next day, the United States declared war on Japan. Four days later, Germany and Italy declared war on the United States.

The role of photography became more important in World War II than in any previous conflict. Thousands of photographers, military and civilian, covered the globe to record the war. Millions of photos were taken. Most

OPPOSITE: Marine Corporal J. Fabian took this picture during the battle of the Marshalls on February 2, 1944. A Japanese soldier waves his arms in surrender while his comrade crawls out from under debris under the watchful eyes of two marines. **LEFT:** This Speed Graphic camera, held by Marine Sergeant Angelo R. Caramico, shows damage from an enemy bullet.

important, war photographers won equal footing with war correspondents. In 1942, a Pulitzer Prize was awarded to a combat photographer for the first time, signaling that combat photography had indeed come of age.

JOE ROSENTHAL

Joe Rosenthal, the photographer who was to take what many consider the greatest combat photo of all time, was born in 1912 in Washington, D.C. He began his photographic career in San Francisco in 1930 with the NEA Service. Before the war, he also worked for the San Francisco *News* and the New York Times–Wide World Photos. Like Mathew Brady, his success as a photographer belied his very poor vision.

When war broke out, Rosenthal was rejected by the draft. Nevertheless, he got into the U.S. Maritime Service as a chief photographer's mate. He served until February 1944 then returned to the Associated Press office in San Francisco. The next month, AP assigned him to the Pacific.

On February 19, 1945, Rosenthal landed with the marines in an assault on the small island of Iwo Jima, which quickly became the scene of vicious fighting.

Rosenthal almost didn't live to make it to Iwo Jima. On the morning of the attack, while climbing from the command ship into a landing ship, he lost his footing and fell into the water between the ships. The ocean was rough, and the assault ship banged repeatedly against the larger ship. Rosenthal watched the two ships closing together over him. They stopped inches short of crushing him, and the marines fished him out. Fortunately, he had just handed his Speed Graphic camera to a marine.

On February 23, Rosenthal heard that some marines were about to raise a flag atop Mount Suribachi, and he and three marine photographers began the steep climb to the top. They ran into four marines on their way down, and one of them, Sergeant Lou Lowery of *Leatherneck* magazine, told Rosenthal that he had already taken several photos of a marine team raising the flag. It seemed foolish at first to duplicate Lowery's pictures, but Rosenthal decided to go up anyway. It was a rugged climb. His account of the ascent appears in John Faber's *Great Moments in News Photography*.

There was still an occasional sharp crack of rifle fire close by and the mountainside had a porcupine appearance of bristling all over, what with machine and antiaircraft guns peering from the dugouts, foxholes, and caves. There was little sign of life from the enemy spots, however.

Rosenthal gives this vivid description of the landing

My landing craft was afloat nearly six hours before the beach was cleared away sufficiently to permit landing at the north beachhead, which was flanked on the right by a cliff bristling with mortars and heavy guns. When the signal came to go in, it was time to check the imagination and keep the eyes on what was going on around, to keep the camera dry and get up the beach as fast as possible, burrow in and size up the picture possibilities.

Because of the . . . explosions around me I could not hear the click of the shutter. Iwo was the hottest beachhead of all and . . . the landings on Guam, Peleliu and Anguar were pale alongside of it.

At one time I hailed a couple of medical corpsmen sweating and sliding along the loose sand bearing a wounded man. [They] let me know with profanity that a picture was the last thing they wanted and would I stick my camera away and really do something in this war . . . . It was the toughest piece of work I have ever done.

The soft sandy footing which led to the terraces up from the shore made for unsteady going, but time and again I was thankful for the ease the sand gave for burrowing in from the too attentive snipers and close bursts of artillery shells. Two or three scoops with my hands were enough to dig a protective depth. Numerous shell craters and abandoned Japanese trenches made good temporary hideouts as we hopped from one to another advance. After a few snapshots of the advancing marines, I maneuvered back and further toward the south where our own wreckage mingled with that of the blasted Japanese equipment along the beach. It was about this time that the medical corpsmen put me to work. They had lost some of their helpers and I was glad to be of any assistance.

From Faber, *Great Moments in News Photography*

Our men were systematically "blowing out" these places and we had to be on our toes to keep clear of our own demolition squads.

As the trail became steeper, our panting progress slowed to a few yards at a time. I began to wonder and hope that this was worth the effort when suddenly over the brow of the topmost ridge we could spy men working with the flagpole they had so laboriously brought up about three quarters of an hour ahead of us.

When Rosenthal reached the top, he found that the marines were taking down the smaller flag that had been photographed by Lowry, and they were getting ready to hoist a large flag in its place.

"I came up and stood by a few minutes until they were ready to swing the flag-bearing pole into position," he wrote. "I crowded back on the inner edge of the volcano's rim, back as far as I could, in order to include all I could into the scene within the angle covered by my camera lens."

To get the angle he wanted, Rosenthal made a small platform of rocks and sandbags that he took from a Japanese machine-gun emplacement. A sergeant—who was later killed in action—took a position nearby and shouted, "I'm not in your way, am I Joe?" Rosenthal yelled, "No—and there it goes!"

He snapped the picture just as the marines raised the flag. It all took about fifteen seconds. The stirring photo won Rosenthal the 1945 Pulitzer Prize. It became a symbol of victory to the nation at a time when the tide of war was running against the United States, both in Europe and in the Pacific. It is still hailed by many as the greatest combat photograph of all time.

According to *Editor & Publisher*, the picture was carried on more front pages than any news photo in history. It stirred a response unprecedented in American press photography. It made a strong impression on Admiral Chester Nimitz, who called it "one of the most extraordinary war photos I have ever seen."

The Gannett newspapers carried the photo with an analysis by an art critic who compared the picture to Leonardo da Vinci's *The Last Supper*, saying: "It is a work finished and complete. Not a thing could be added by a consummate craftsman." The *Dansville* [Virginia] *Register* likened it to the painting of Washington crossing the Delaware. The *New York Sun* saw a striking similarity in feeling with the famous painting *The Spirit of '76*. The *Louisville Courier Journal* called it "the best job of the war." The *Boston Post* declared, "Newspaper tradition is made greater by this feat." It inspired many poems and became the model for a monument that now stands near Washington, D.C. Its likeness was issued on a postage stamp to commemorate the marines.

A useful perspective was provided by *Editor & Publisher* in an editorial of March 17, 1945;

This photo is a living tribute to the civilian war photographers of the American press.... It is a tribute...to many others who have been wounded, performing their job of photographing the war up front so we at home can see what it is like. Rosenthal got "the greatest picture," but others have undergone the same dangers and

As this tank crew surrendered to American GIs in Belgium, one of the German soldiers threw a grenade, wounding *Life* magazine photographer George Silk.

hardships doing the same job rewarded only by heartbreak when circumstances of time and distance prevented their having similar success.

FRANK E. NOEL

Another combat photographer who captured a Pulitzer Prize was Frank E. Noel, an Associated Press photographer from the New York bureau. Born in 1905 in Dalhard, Texas, Noel started his career when he was twenty years old, with the *Chicago Daily News*, and stayed with that paper three years. He then worked for the *Washington Post* for one year, quitting in 1929.

During the Mexican Revolution, Noel freelanced. He next worked three years on the *Wichita* (Kansas) *Eagle*, two years on the *Kansas City Star*, and for a few months on the *Oklahoma City News* as chief photographer. In 1937, he joined the Associated Press at Buffalo, New York. He followed the king and queen of Britain on their tour of the United States in 1939. He then worked at AP bureaus in Atlanta and Miami. In September 1941, he was transferred to New York for foreign service.

On December 7, 1941, Noel found himself on assignment in Singapore. To escape the Japanese advance, he started out by ship for India, but the ship was torpedoed near Sumatra. Only Noel and twenty-seven of the ship's company of seventy-seven made it to the lifeboats. The small boats drifted in the Indian Ocean for weeks, and it was during this ordeal at sea that Noel took the photo that won him a Pulitzer Prize in 1943. Noel himself was in mortal danger at the time, but he managed to snap an unforgettable picture of a thirsty East Indian sailor on another lifeboat pleading for a drink of water.

Noel and the other survivors reached safety at Padang, Sumatra, more than six weeks after their ship

BELOW: This dramatic appeal for water by a seaman was taken by Associated Press photographer Frank Noel in January 1942 as he drifted in a lifeboat near Sumatra after his ship was torpedoed in the Indian Ocean. The picture won the 1943 Pulitzer Prize.

OPPOSITE: Joe Rosenthal's picture of the second flag being raised by marines on Mount Suribachi, a 550-foot [167m] peak on Iwo Jima, became the best known of all combat pictures. The raising of the first flag was photographed by two marine photographers: Bob Campbell and Lou Lowery. Rosenthal sent a copy of this photo to Lowery with the notation "To the photographer who got there first."

went down. He returned to the United States to recuperate. In June 1945, he was back on assignment in Rome. Noel then became an AP troubleshooter who could be counted on to take excellent photos.

In May 1948, he covered the Palestine conflict; in 1949, he was sent to Berlin; when the Korean conflict broke out, he was there within a month. In 1950, while in action on the front lines, he was captured by the Communists near Changjin reservoir and was not released until almost three years later.

He returned once again to New York, where he worked on the wire photo desk. In May 1966, after twenty-eight eventful years with AP, he retired.

FRANK FILAN

Another man to win a Pulitzer Prize with a dramatic war photo was AP photographer Frank Filan. Filan took his prize-winning picture during the capture of the island of Tarawa. It showed marines examining the ruins of a Japanese stronghold, with the bodies of Japanese soldiers strewn among the rubble.

Filan was not only a great war photographer; he was an authentic war hero. He landed on Tarawa in heavy surf with the first marine assault wave. He jumped into the water with the marines about 150 yards [135m] from the beach. Enemy fire was heavy. When a marine near him was hit and appeared to be drowning, Filan stripped off his bulky equipment, picked up the bleeding man, and carried him to the beach. Small wonder that when a colleague later asked about the best way to take pictures of island fighting, Filan said, "I told him the main thing was to get to the beach without being shot.... There are pictures on all sides, and you merely have to shoot them."

During the first ten days on Tarawa, Filan braved enemy fire scores of times to rescue wounded marines. For three days, he went without food or water. Fleet Admiral Chester Nimitz gave him commendations for "inspired devotion to duty." But as a photographer, Filan was desperate. He was stranded on an island without equipment, in the center of a sensational story. It wasn't until three days after the beachhead was established that a Coast Guard officer came to his rescue with a camera and some film. He often praised the Coast Guard for helping him win his prize.

The Coast Guard came to my aid when I needed it most. If it hadn't happened to me I wouldn't believe it. Only a fellow newspaperman can appreciate what a nightmare I was living, to be in on one of the best stories in years with no means to cover it.

Filan served three years in combat areas. He made sixteen amphibious landings, with dozens of close scrapes with death. Not all his narrow escapes were in war zones; while covering an inspection tour of army flying fields on the West Coast in 1942, the plane he was in collided in mid-air with another plane near Victorville, California. Just before the plane crashed and burned, he bailed out to safety; but for several hours, he was listed as one of the victims. Dazed and suffering from spine and head injuries, he wandered in the desert until dawn, when he was found.

In 1946, while Filan was covering the Chinese Communist revolt against Chaing Kai-Shek, his jeep overturned and he fractured his arm. He was brought back to the United States and reassigned to the Los Angeles bureau, where he covered the Hollywood scene.

In 1951, he became seriously ill. He died in Los Angeles in July 1952, at the age of forty-seven.

BERT BRANDT

The best-known Acme (later, United Press International) photographer was Bert Brandt. Brandt first covered the Italian campaign, and he felt his best pictures came out of that assignment. During the battle for Lagone, for example, Brandt had moved ahead of the troops to a patch of rocky ground. A burst of enemy fire made him dive for cover. The terrain was so hard that he could not dig in, so he had to lie flat and hope for the best. It was a clear night, and Brandt decided to try to take pictures using only the light of the moon and of exploding shells. Luckily, the light was enough, and the resulting pictures were some of the most dramatic that were taken during the entire war.

After the Allies took Rome, Brandt was assigned to England. He landed with the marines on D-Day, and his pictures of the Normandy invasion were the first to be published in the U.S.

ANDREW LOPEZ

Another Acme photographer, Andrew Lopez, also covered the D-Day invasion. Lopez landed in Normandy six days after the first troops. During the American advance through France, he was riding toward the front in a jeep with a Reuters photographer and a driver when a German shell hit the jeep. The Reuters man was killed instantly. Lopez and the driver, both injured, jumped from the wreckage and got into a ditch, still under enemy fire. They stayed in the ditch until dark, then stumbled into the woods, where they rubbed sulfanilamide into each other's wounds to prevent infection.

For two days they had no food or water, but on the morning of the third day, they spotted a Frenchwoman in a field milking a cow. They crawled toward her, and with broken French and sign language, they made her understand who they were and that they were hungry. The woman left, but another woman returned with bread and a pail of milk for them. That night they hiked to another town. Suddenly, dogs started barking and French soldiers began shooting. The jeep driver was killed, but Lopez man-

OPPOSITE: An American B-24 Liberator trails smoke after a bombing run on Vienna, Austria on October 13, 1944.

BELOW: Front-line photographers rush negatives of the fall of Rome to a mobile photo lab on June 11, 1944, while one soldier types up the captions.

OPPOSITE:

Seemingly oblivious
to an old German
woman who surveys
the ruins of her home
in despair, members
of the 180th Infantry
Regiment, Forty-fifth
Division, XV Corps of
the U.S. Seventh
Army continue their
advance through
Bensheim, Germany
on March 27, 1945.

aged to shout that he was an American. He was taken into a house and given food, water, and first aid. The next day, he was taken to an American post where the shrapnel was dug out of his face, arms, and shoulder. A few days later, he was back in combat, photographing the First Army.

Near St. Lô, France, Lopez went with some officers to the top of a captured enemy fort built into the side of a mountain. While he was snapping pictures of the American troops advancing below, some Germans who were hiding in the fort opened fire on his group. The Germans were quickly captured when the troops arrived, however, and Lopez was not hurt. He also covered the fall of Paris, the capture of the Siegfried Line, and some of General MacArthur's campaign in the South Pacific. He was commended for bravery for aiding wounded troops under fire.

SAMUEL SCHULMAN

Samuel Schulman, the best-known photographer for International News Pictures, won his fame mainly because of two men: President Franklin D. Roosevelt and reporter Bob Considine.

Schulman was born in 1903, the son of a Brooklyn rabbi. He says he got "the tramp's toss" out of Hebrew Technical Institute in Brooklyn because he spent too much time reading biographies and too little time studying calculus.

At seventeen, he got a job as a copyboy on the New York *American*, where such famous reporters as Damon Runyon, Arthur Brisbane, and Gene Fowler worked. Schulman, attracted to news photography, bought a $90 Speed Graphic, and two years later, thanks to his hard work, became a staff photographer.

His pay soared from twelve dollars a week to fifteen, and he was soon covering major assignments for both the *American* and International News Pictures. He was eventually assigned to the prestigious beat at the White House, where he photographed Calvin Coolidge, Herbert Hoover, and Franklin D. Roosevelt.

He took FDR's photo at the White House on innumerable occasions. He even taught the president how to operate a Speed Graphic. During the war, when Schulman was sent overseas, the president often would look up at the photographers around him and ask,

"Where's Sammy?" Bob Considine, a famous INS writer, used that phrase as the title of an autobiography of Schulman that he edited in 1943.

At the outbreak of the war, Schulman was assigned to North Africa. Before leaving, he did something that many men do before going into battle—he wrote a note to a friend.

"If anything happens to me," he wrote, "there are some important papers in my locker at the office, including a letter marked 'Instructions.' Please do what it says." Later he wrote, "I leave that letter of instructions at the office all the time. It has to do with what I want done with my stuff, if my luck runs out."

He also covered many campaigns in Europe, and of combat photography he wrote, "If, in peace, a picture is worth 10,000 words, a war picture must be worth 100,000 for it conveys at a single glance an emotion which takes so many, many words to convey—the emotion of horror."

ROBERT LEE BRYANT

Robert Lee Bryant covered the Pacific and China-Burma-India Theater for INP. Bryant joined the organization five days after Pearl Harbor and was the company's first man assigned to combat. He claimed that his most exciting mission was with General Merrill's Marauders behind Japanese lines.

General Stillwell gave Bryant permission to join up with that outfit if he could get to the scene of operations.

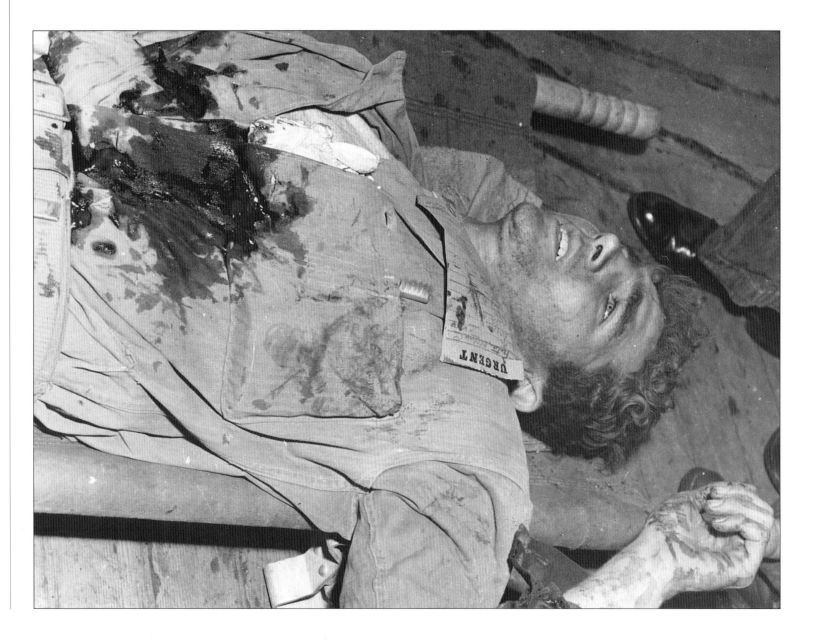

To do this, Bryant arranged to bail out over a spot near the Marauders' headquarters. The pilot, however, decided to land on a beach that turned out to be miles from the point of rendezvous. Bryant had to travel for weeks on horseback through dangerous jungle to find the base. A detachment that tried to make the same journey a few weeks later was wiped out in a Japanese ambush. Bryant got by with dysentery, malaria, a wrenched knee, a twisted ankle, and other minor ills.

CARL MYDANS

More than any other combat photographer, *Life*'s Carl Mydans was in the thick of World War II from beginning to end. Born in Boston in 1913, Mydans graduated from Boston University's College of Communication, then worked as a reporter on the *Boston Globe* and the *Boston Herald* and eventually on the *American Banker* in New York, where he took up photography. His pictures for a government agency caught the eye of Henry Luce, who in 1936 had just begun to publish *Life*. Mydans joined the staff as one of its first photographers. He married *Life* researcher Shelley Smith, and for the next ten years—until their first child was born—they worked as a photo-reporter team. As the first of *Life*'s "roving correspondents," they traveled through England, Finland, and the Continent, photographing preparations for war. In 1941, they went on to Burma, Malaya, and the Philippines.

By December 1942, Guadalcanal, in the Solomon Islands, was firmly in American hands. This photo shows the fate of some of the Japanese jungle fighters who defended the island.

OPPOSITE: The destroyer USS *Shaw* and other ships explode after being hit by Japanese bombs at Pearl Harbor on December 7, 1941.

BELOW: Lieutenant Donald Mittle Laedt, who commanded a photo unit on New Britain, is shown on June 20, 1944 as he prepares to photograph the fighting.

They were captured in January 1942, when the Japanese army entered Manila, and along with all other British and Americans who were taken prisoner, they were locked up in a makeshift prison in a barren university building. When the Japanese discovered that Mydans was a famous photographer, they offered to free him and his wife if he would take pictures for them. Mydans refused, and he and his wife remained prisoners for almost two years. They were released in October 1943.

After he recuperated from his prison experience, Mydans was sent to North Africa, then to Italy, and then to southern France. He was ordered back to the Far East in September 1944. He landed with the marines on Luzon and, ironically, photographed the very camp in which he and his wife had been held captive. He drew the only photographer's spot on General MacArthur's flagship, the cruiser *Boise*. He was one of the few American photographers aboard the battleship *Missouri* in Tokyo Bay at the formal surrender of Japan.

In 1948, he covered the French forces in Indochina. Two years later, he shot assignments in Korea, and his photos and articles there won him the title of "the foot-slogger's photographer."

OPPOSITE: Sergeant Robert E. Follendorf took this picture of Corpsman Hubert Hammond giving first aid to the wounded Sergeant David G. Christian, one of fifty marine photographers on Iwo Jima.

BELOW: *Life* photographer Carl Mydans in Finland covering the Soviet-Finnish war of 1939–40.

In his autobiography, *More Than Meets the Eye*, Carl Mydans took a philosophical look at his career

Sometime during my last years in high school, journalism caught my imagination....And I have since credited myself with selecting the most satisfying and exciting profession, for in the pursuit of journalism, perhaps more than any other profession, one comes closer to and lives more intimately and imaginatively with the world he loves. This is especially true of photojournalism; for here one joins mind and hand, and here the reporter must always come in closest contact with his subject....A writer may get his story of bridge building from the ground. But the camera has to be above the men. No great combat picture was ever made in a headquarters briefing. And no camera that was ever late for an assault was ever "filled in" later by comrades in journalism or by survivors of the action. The camera must always be there. And behind it there must always be a man's eye, and a soul.

W. EUGENE SMITH

Remarkably, only one *Life* staffer, noted photographer W. Eugene Smith, was seriously wounded in action. Smith first covered the war in the Atlantic, then went to the South Pacific, where he was in thirteen invasions and twenty-six carrier combat missions. He was hit on Okinawa by a Japanese shell fragment while photographing an essay, "A Day in the Life of a Front-Line Soldier." The fragment hit his head, cut both cheeks, knocked out several teeth, injured his tongue, and broke his hand. "I forgot to duck," he said, "but I got a wonderful shot of those who did.... My policy of standing up when the others are down finally caught up with me."

MARGARET BOURKE-WHITE

Margaret Bourke-White, *Life*'s first staff photographer, was also the first woman accredited by the U.S. armed forces as a combat photographer. She was consistently in the thick of the fighting, repeatedly risking her life to get good photos. On the way to her first combat assignment, in North Africa, her ship was torpedoed and sunk. Undaunted, she spent two years on the Italian peninsula. She covered the siege of Moscow. She crossed the Rhine with Patton's army. She took pictures of Germany's concentration camps and bombed-out cities. On an aerial mission over Germany, she barely escaped when Nazi planes attacked her unarmed observation plane. Many of her photos were taken for the armed forces, and Secretary of War Patterson expressed official appreciation for her "outstanding and conspicuous service as an accredited war correspondent."

ROBERT CAPA

One more civilian photographer deserves special attention: Robert Capa, who has been described by many people, including photo historian Peter Pollack, as "the greatest combat photographer of his time."

Born in 1913 in Hungary, Capa was strangely fascinated by wars. At the age of twenty-two, while covering the Spanish Civil War, he took an unforgettable picture of a Spanish Loyalist falling to the battlefield at the instant of his death by gunfire.

Capa came to the United States at the onset of World War II to work for *Life*. He soon returned to Europe to cover North Africa, Normandy, and the Liberation. In the spring of 1947, he was instrumental in founding Magnum Photos, which grew to be one of the leading picture agencies in the world. Later, he photographed the Korean conflict. He met his death on the battlefield, in Vietnam in 1954, after spending eighteen of his forty-one years photographing combat.

Of the Normandy invasion, Capa wrote

At 4 A.M. we were assembled on the open deck. The invasion barges were swinging on the cranes, ready to be lowered. Waiting for the light, the two thousand men stood in perfect silence; whatever they were thinking, it was some kind of prayer.

I too stood very quietly. I was thinking a little bit of everything; of green fields, pink clouds, grazing sheep, all the good times, and very much of getting the best pictures of the day. None of us was at all impatient, and we wouldn't have minded standing in the darkness for a very long time. But the sun had no way of knowing that this day was different from all others, and rose on its usual schedule. The first-wavers stumbled into their barges, and—as if on slow-moving elevators—we descended into the sea. The sea was rough and we were wet before our barge pushed away from the mother ship.

In no time, the men started to puke. But this was a polite as well as a carefully prepared invasion, and little paper bags had been provided for the purpose....

The flat bottom of our barge hit the earth of France. The boatswain lowered the steel-covered barge front, and there, between the grotesque designs of steel obstacles sticking out of the water, was a thin line of sand covered with smoke—our Europe, the Easy Red beach.

My beautiful France looked sordid and uninviting, and a German machine-gun, spitting bullets around the barge, fully spoiled my return. The men from my barge waded in the water. Waist-deep, with rifles ready to shoot, with the invasion obstacles and the smoking beach in the background—this was good enough for the photographer. I paused for a moment on the gangplank to take my first real picture of the invasion. The boatswain, who was in an understandable hurry to get the hell out of there, mistook my picture-taking attitude for explicable hesitation, and helped me make up my mind with a well-aimed kick in the rear. The water was cold and the beach still more than a hundred yards [90m] away. The bullets tore holes in the water around me, and I made for the nearest steel obstacle. A soldier got there at the same time, and for a few minutes we shared its cover. He took the waterproofing off his rifle, and began to shoot without much aiming at the smoke-ridden beach. The sound of his rifle gave him enough courage to move forward and he left the obstacle to me. It was a foot larger now, and I felt safe enough to take pictures of the other guys hiding just like I was....

I finished my pictures, and the sea was cold in my trousers. Reluctantly, I tried to move away from my steel pole, but the bullets chased me back every time. Fifty yards [45m] ahead of me, one of our half-burnt amphibious tanks stuck out of the water and offered me my next cover. I sized up the situation. There was little future for the elegant raincoat heavy on my arm. I dropped it and made for the tank. Between floating bodies I reached it, paused for a few more pictures, and gathered my guts for the last jump to the beach.

Now the Germans played on all their instruments and I could not find any hole between the shells and the bullets that blocked the last twenty-five yards [22.5m] to the beach. I just stayed behind my tank, repeating a little sentence from my Spanish Civil War days, *Es una cosa muy seria. Es una cosa muy seria.* —This is a very serious business.

The tide was coming in, and now the water reached the farewell letter to my family in my breast pocket. Behind the human cover of the last two guys, I reached the beach. I threw myself flat and my lips touched the earth of France. I had no desire to kiss it....

Saint Laurent-sur-Mer must have been at one time a drab, cheap resort for the vacationing French schoolteachers. Now, on June 6, 1944, it was the ugliest beach in the whole world. Exhausted from the water and the fear, we lay flat on a small strip of wet sand between the sea and the barbed wire. The slant of the beach gave us some protection, so long as we lay flat, from the machine-gun and rifle bullets, but the tide pushed us against the barbed wire, where the guns were enjoying open season. I crawled on my stomach over to my friend Larry, the Irish padre of the regiment, who could swear better than any amateur. He growled at me, "You damn half-Frenchy. If you don't like it here, why the hell did you come back?" Thus comforted by religion, I took out my second Contax camera and began to shoot without raising my head.

From the air "Easy Red" must have looked like an open tin of sardines. Shooting from the sardine's angle, the foreground of my pictures was filled with wet boots

and green faces. Above the boots and faces, my picture frames were filled with shrapnel smoke; burnt tanks and sinking barges formed my background. Larry had a dry cigarette. I reached in my hip pocket for my silver flask and offered it to him. He tilted his head sideways and took a swig from the corner of his mouth. Before returning the bottle he gave it to my other chum, the Jewish medic, who very successfully imitated Larry's technique. The corner of my mouth was good enough for me too.

The next mortar shell exploded between the barbed wire and the sea, and every piece of shrapnel found a man's body. The Irish priest and the Jewish doctor were the first to stand up on the "Easy Red" beach. I shot the picture. The next shell fell even closer. I didn't dare to take my eyes off the finder of my Contax and frantically shot frame after frame. Half a minute later, my camera jammed—my roll was finished. I reached in my bag for a new roll, and my wet shaking hands ruined the roll before I could insert it in the camera.

I paused for a moment...and then I had it bad.

The empty camera trembled in my hands. It was a new kind of fear shaking my body from toe to hair, and twisting my face. I unhooked my shovel and tried to dig a hole. The shovel hit stone under the sand and I hurled it away. The men around me lay motionless.

Only the dead on the water line rolled with waves. An LCI braved the fire, and medics with red crosses painted on their helmets poured from it. I did not think and I didn't decide it. I just stood up and ran toward the boat. I stepped into the sea between two bodies and the water reached to my neck. The riptide hit my body and every wave slapped my face under my helmet. I held my cameras high above my head, and suddenly I knew that I was running away. I tried to turn but couldn't face the beach, and told myself, "I am just going to dry my hands on that boat."

I reached the boat. The last medics were just getting out. I climbed aboard. As I reached the deck I felt a shock, and suddenly was all covered with feathers. I thought, "What is this? Is somebody killing chickens?" Then I saw that the superstructure had been shot away and that the feathers were the stuffing from the kapok jackets of the men that had been blown up. The skipper was crying. His assistant had been blown up all over him, and he was a mess.

Our boat was listing and we slowly pulled away from the beach to try and reach the mother ship before we sank. I went down to the engine room, dried my hands and put fresh films in both cameras. I got back up on deck again in time to take one last picture of the smoke-covered beach. Then I took some shots of the crew giving transfusions on the open deck. An invasion barge came alongside and took us off the sinking boat. The transfer of the badly wounded on the heavy seas was a difficult business. I took no more pictures. I was busy lifting stretchers. The barge brought us to the USS *Chase*, the very boat I had left only six hours before. On the *Chase*, the last wave of the Sixteenth Infantry was just being lowered, but the decks were already full with returning wounded and dead.

This was my last chance to return to the beach. I did not go. The mess boys who had served our coffee in white jackets with white gloves at three in the morning were covered with blood and were sewing the dead in white sacks.

Seven days later, I learned that the pictures I had taken on "Easy Red" were the best of the invasion. But the excited darkroom assistant, while drying the negatives, had turned on too much heat and the emulsions had melted and run down before the eyes of the London office. Out of 106 pictures in all, only eight were salvaged.

From Capa, *Images of War*

Military photographers played an important role in World War II. When war erupted in Europe in 1939, long before the United States became involved, a flood of combat photos poured out of Allied and Axis countries. American military leaders were freshly impressed by the strategic values of such pictures, and training programs were stepped up accordingly.

Military photography in the European theater mushroomed from a small beginning a few weeks after Pearl Harbor to one of the largest photographic operations in the world. In typical military fashion, each organization sent out its own photographers: army, navy, marines, air force, Red Cross, American Field Service, "Stars and Stripes," War Shipping Administration, Psychological Warfare Branch, Army Medical Museum, and the Navy Surgeon General's Office, to name a few.

Shortly after Pearl Harbor, however, the War Department formed a "still picture pool" whereby civilian camera coverage was put on the basis of pooled manpower, so as not to duplicate assignments. The aim was to get as many photographers as possible into as many areas as were accessible, and then share the results. All combat pictures, military and civilian, were made available to everyone.

EDWARD STEICHEN

Some of the most outstanding photographs of the war were taken by a navy unit commanded by Captain Edward Steichen, of World War I fame. Steichen personally recruited some of the country's top professional photographers, and assigned them to where the fighting was the heaviest. To minimize the possibility that their film might be ruined by mistake, he made sure that their prints were developed by other professionals. Steichen himself kept close track of the pictures so that none would be lost.

Steichen was sixty-one years old when World War II broke out, but he was eager to get into the middle of it. The feelings he had had on the night of the armistice had not changed: "if we could really photograph war as it was...in all its monstrous actuality, that could be a great deterrent for war." The army, however, took one look at his age and refused his offer to reenlist. But he was not to be dissuaded. He turned to the navy, and convinced the brass that he would be an asset to them; he was allowed to assemble a team of photographers to cover naval aviation.

Steichen was promoted to captain in 1944 and put in charge of all navy combat photography. His military decorations from World War I and World War II include the Distinguished Service Citation, Chevalier of Legion of Honor, and the Distinguished Service Medal. The latter is the most significant medal ever awarded to an American combat photographer.

JERRY JOSWICK

The most dramatic and dangerous photographic mission of the war—as Robert Capa's account makes clear—was D-Day, June 6, 1944, when the Allies launched their invasion of occupied France.

Nearly six hundred photographers were involved in the mission. Almost half the Signal Corps photographers were killed. Sergeant Jerry Joswick, a highly decorated army photographer from Chicago who never refused an assignment, was there that morning, ready to leave his assault craft by jeep.

He carried his Speed Graphic in a waterproof bag around his neck. (Many photographers, especially in the tropics, found that condoms were the most effective way to waterproof their cameras.)

According to Joswick,

We were going in. The barge picked her way among the sunken and listing vessels, only one of the dozens of assault craft that sped along like water bugs. Geysers leaped between us. On shore, slowly enlarging, was the several-mile-long tangle of tank obstacles, barbed wire and flashing machine-gun and shell fire.

The maw dropped open. Jeep motors revved up. The jeep lunged down the ramp...into twenty feet [6m] of water. Pulled down by all my equipment, I sank to the bottom. Coughing up sea water, I lay on the beach with wavelets pushing, tugging me back, pushing me forward again. How I got there still loaded with equipment—whether I swam or was rescued by someone now gone—I have never known.

While I was in this state of deep discouragement, I received a telephone call from the Navy Department in Washington asking me if I would be interested in photographing for the navy. I almost crawled through the telephone wires with eagerness. I replied that it so happened I had an appointment in Washington the next day. I took a night train and, at an early hour, turned up at naval headquarters. I was heartily welcomed by Commander Arthur Doyle and was introduced to Captain A.W. Radford, who was then in command of training for naval aviators.

When I walked into Radford's office, I saw a look of surprise on his face. He had apparently not been informed that I was no longer a young man. Just then his telephone rang, and while he was talking I was saying to myself, "Boy, you've got to talk fast now." And the moment Captain Radford hung up, I started talking fast, telling him about my service in World War I and stressing my personal experiences under General Mitchell. This seemed to interest him very much, and I followed up quickly with a proposition.

I told him I would like to head up a small unit of half a dozen photographers, commissioned by the navy, to photograph the story of naval aviation during the war. This project interested Captain Radford. He took me to the assistant secretary of the Navy for Air to introduce me and to present the idea to him. Again I saw the shocked expression at my age, this time on the Secretary's face. Finally, he said to Captain Radford, "Well, if you really want him, I guess it's all right."

Captain Radford answered, as solemnly as a groom in a marriage ceremony, "I do."

I immediately started assembling a group of young photographers who were very divergent in their work and personalities. It took only a few weeks to select enough men to get the work of the unit organized, but gradually, we added more photographers. Eventually, the unit consisted of Wayne Miller, Charles Kerlee, Fenno Jacobs, Horace Bristol, Victor Jorgensen, Barrett Gallagher, and John Swope, all commissioned in the navy, and Paul Dorsey,

assigned to the unit from the Marine Corps. Navy Lieutenant Willard Mace served as executive assistant. In civilian life, the photographers had worked variously in journalism, documentary photography, illustration, advertising, and marine photography. Off duty, almost every one of them sooner or later came to me separately and said he understood why he had been chosen for the job, but he couldn't understand why some of the others had been.

I soon found that we were a rather irregular unit in the organizational setup of the navy, and at first we met with opposition from the navy's regular photographic service. Captain Radford, who soon became Admiral Radford, cleared this away and obtained for our photographers the freedom of movement and action necessary for good photography, but unprecedented in the navy.

On our first job, we overcame a long-standing navy taboo. Before the war, it was considered undignified for an officer to carry a camera for making official photographs. All this work was assigned to noncommissioned personnel. But at the first naval air station our unit was assigned to photograph, each man turned up with several cameras slung around his shoulders and the usual kit bag of film and accessories. We were all officers, but no one challenged our right to carry a camera, then or at any time during the service.

I sent the men out on missions to various ships, usually aircraft carriers, since naval aviation was our job, and they all turned in exciting pictures. But curiously enough, although each man, in coming into the unit, had expressed enthusiasm for the freedom he would have in doing the kind of photography he wanted, he would invariably come to me before going on an assignment and ask, "Now, just what do you want me to do?"

One of Steichen's men photographed crewmen on the aircraft carrier USS *Bunker Hill* running for cover after the ship is hit by two kamikaze planes on May 11, 1945.

BELOW: A radioactive mushroom cloud billows some twenty thousand feet [6,100m] over Hiroshima, Japan on August 6, 1945 after the first offensive use of the atomic bomb, dropped from the B-29 Enola Gay. This picture was taken with a K-20 camera by Sergeant George R. Caron.

OPPOSITE: A comrade ducks for cover as a U.S. marine, armed with a Thompson submachine gun, fires on a Japanese sniper near the town of Shuri on Okinawa.

GEORGE R. CARON

The closing act of World War II—and the dawn of a hideous new era of war—was photographed on August 5, 1945. Photographic Officer Captain Jerome J. Ossip of the 509th Composite Group was ready to take off in a lone B-29, the Enola Gay, to record the first use of an atomic bomb against an enemy. He loaded and set up his K-20 camera in the plane, but at the last minute before takeoff, the pilot, Major Paul W. Tibbets, Jr., told him he could not go. So to preserve the event on film, Ossip gave the loaded camera to the tail gunner, Sergeant George R. Caron, and told him how to use it. When the bomb was dropped, Caron began snapping pictures. He used the entire fifty-exposure roll as the enormous mushroom cloud billowed up from below. Captain Ossip stood by nervously with Generals Carl Spaatz, Curtis LeMay, and Nathan Twining for the return of the bomber and the pictures of the explosion. The roll produced picture after incredible picture of the blast, and on August 11, one of the photos was released by the military to newspapers all over the world—a world that was suddenly very different.

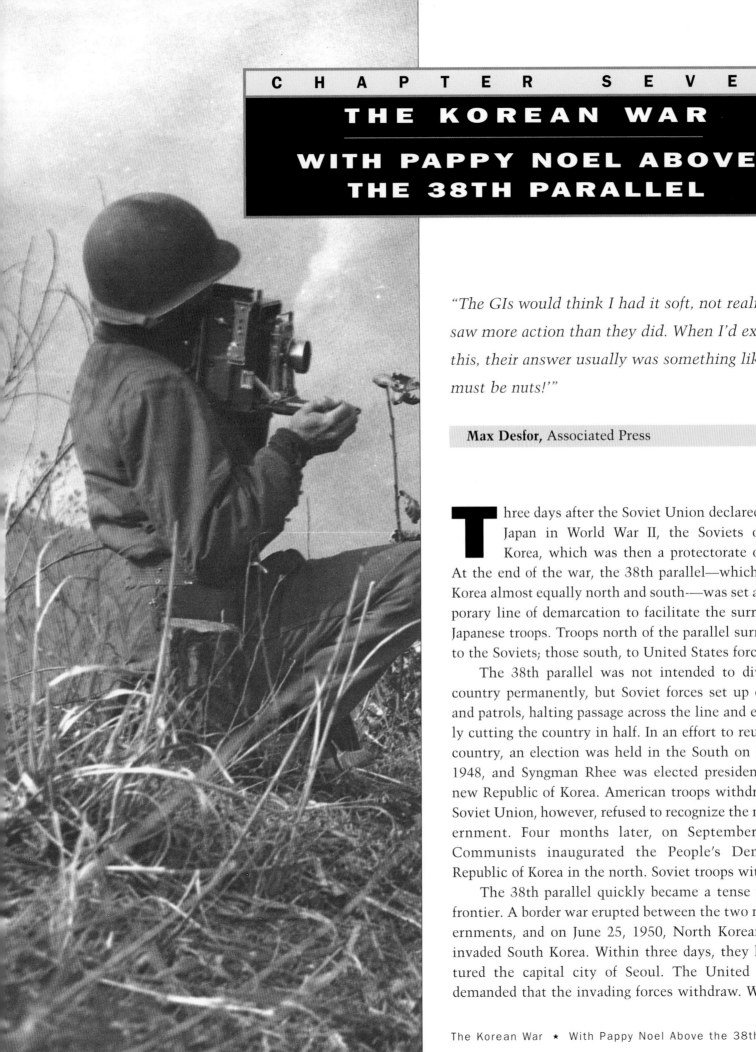

CHAPTER SEVEN

THE KOREAN WAR

WITH PAPPY NOEL ABOVE THE 38TH PARALLEL

"The GIs would think I had it soft, not realizing I saw more action than they did. When I'd explain this, their answer usually was something like, 'You must be nuts!'"

Max Desfor, Associated Press

Three days after the Soviet Union declared war on Japan in World War II, the Soviets occupied Korea, which was then a protectorate of Japan. At the end of the war, the 38th parallel—which divides Korea almost equally north and south-—was set as a temporary line of demarcation to facilitate the surrender of Japanese troops. Troops north of the parallel surrendered to the Soviets; those south, to United States forces.

The 38th parallel was not intended to divide the country permanently, but Soviet forces set up outposts and patrols, halting passage across the line and effectively cutting the country in half. In an effort to reunify the country, an election was held in the South on May 10, 1948, and Syngman Rhee was elected president of the new Republic of Korea. American troops withdrew. The Soviet Union, however, refused to recognize the new government. Four months later, on September 9, the Communists inaugurated the People's Democratic Republic of Korea in the north. Soviet troops withdrew.

The 38th parallel quickly became a tense political frontier. A border war erupted between the two new governments, and on June 25, 1950, North Korean troops invaded South Korea. Within three days, they had captured the capital city of Seoul. The United Nations demanded that the invading forces withdraw. When the

OPPOSITE: Famed war photographer David Douglas Duncan took this picture in sub-zero weather at the Pusan Perimeter in Korea in October 1950. He used a Leica IIIC camera with a Nikkor 50mm, f1.4 lens.
LEFT: Cpl. Donald Miller of Flint, Michigan, a Twenty-fourth Signal Company photographer in Korea, focuses his Speed Graphic on the action on April 7, 1951.

Machine gunners fire from an emplacement overlooking a bridge somewhere in Korea on July 20, 1950.

demand was ignored, the Security Council recommended that the members of the U.N. help South Korea repel the Communist attack.

On June 27, President Harry Truman sent in American air and naval forces to support the South Korean troops. He named General Douglas MacArthur to command the U.N. forces. Then came three years of bitter fighting that claimed 22,359 American lives. The Korean truce was signed on July 25, 1953, at Panmunjom. The United States hailed the armistice as a triumph for collective security under the U.N., while the Communists saw it as a victory over capitalistic imperialism.

MAX DESFOR

The Korean War produced another Pulitzer Prize-winning combat photographer, Max Desfor, who spent eight of his sixteen years with AP in battle zones. Born in Brooklyn in 1913, Desfor began studying photography while attending Brooklyn College. He joined AP in 1933 as a messenger boy. It took him five years to become a photographer with the Baltimore AP bureau, but from then on promotions came quickly. In 1939, he was promoted to the Washington bureau. In 1941, he won first prize in the White House News Photographers Association contest. In 1944, AP sent him overseas to cover World War II, where he photographed action on both Guam and Okinawa. He

was with the marines on the first landing in Japan and covered the early phases of the occupation. He was one of the AP photographers who covered the surrender of Japan on the battleship *Missouri* in Tokyo Bay. He went on to work in a variety of trouble spots, including India, Kashmir, Burma, Afghanistan, Indonesia, and Pakistan.

Two weeks after the Korean conflict began, Desfor was on the front lines with the U.S. Twenty-fourth Infantry. In December, the Chinese Communists joined the North Korean troops, and the U.N. forces fell back. During the retreat, Desfor took the photo that was awarded the 1951 Pulitzer Prize. Desfor remained in Korea until the truce was signed. He managed to be in on every major engagement, and one time even parachuted behind enemy lines with one of the first waves of the Eighteenth Regimental combat team. He was totally inexperienced in jumping, but his philosophy was, "If a story's worth covering, it's worth any personal risk involved."

Max Desfor recalls taking the shot that won the Pulitzer Prize

We had to get out; our troops could no longer hold the capital city of Pyong-Yang. I hopped into a jeep with reporters Tom Lambert of the AP and Homer Bigart of the *New York Times*. The only way to cross the Taedong River was with the military over a pontoon bridge. Reaching the far side we went downriver looking for stories.

I'll never forget the sight as long as I live. We came to a huge bridge which had been bombed and had fallen into the icy river. Crossing over bits of jagged metal were hundreds of people, crawling like ants through the girders. They were half frozen, it being the dead of winter. Some had fallen into the freezing water, and were trying to reach safety. Others clung to the twisted metal in sheer exhaustion. I jumped out of the jeep and ran out on the slippery bed as far as I could go on our side of the bridge. It ended abruptly with a drop of fifty feet [15m] to the water's edge. I must have made four or five shots. All I could think of was the fortitude of these poor miserable souls as they fled from capture and Communist control.

—From Faber, *Great Moments in News Photography*

Associated Press photographer Max Desfor won the 1951 Pulitzer Prize for this photo showing Pyong-Yang residents fleeing in freezing weather over the shattered girders of the city bridge on December 4, 1950.

Desfor felt that Korea was much harder to cover than World War II:

World War II was organized and Korea wasn't. From the very first in Korea we were on our own. When we had to get our films back to an airport, we had to hitchhike a ride. Then we'd have to talk the pilot into flying the films to Tokyo for development. Luckily, despite all these problems, things worked out all right.

FRANK E. NOEL

Frank "Pappy" Noel, a World War II Pulitzer Prize winner, was also among those sent by AP to Korea. On December 1, 1950, when he was forty-five years old, Noel was with a convoy of marines near the Changjin reservoir in northeast Korea, trying to reach an isolated regiment. The marines never reached their goal; North Korean troops cut them off, and most of the marines were killed or captured. Noel was among the captured. The next day, when AP reporter Stan Swinton got the news, he wrote, "Don't write off Pappy Noel. He has seen a lot of war and any number of tight spots. I am betting that 'Pappy' will come back—probably with exclusive pictures."

A year later, five members of AP's Tokyo bureau decided to send Noel a camera for Christmas. The details were worked out a few days later with three Communist correspondents at Panmunjom, and the plan was soon given official approval. The arrangements were kept secret in order not to alert competing newsmen. AP dubbed the project "Operation Father Christmas."

On January 2, 1952, AP headquarters in New York got the following cable from the Tokyo bureau:

"Sent Father Christmas package including Speed Graphic. Under plan. Pappy will make pictures present location for Associated only. Send Tokyo via various couriers whose reliability already proven. Realize this gamble but looks hopeful from here."

New York replied, "Resch [General News Photo Editor Al Resch] joins appreciation for fatherly report and best wishes for its success."

Three weeks later Tokyo wired New York:

"Christmas package in hand being carried by Schutz [Bob Schutz, staff photographer] due Tokyo late tonight."

Although Noel's film was censored, the Communists allowed seven pictures to be transmitted by radio photo to the United States. Noel became the first prisoner of war to release to the outside world pictures of life in a prison camp.

Headlines in American newspapers read: "Exclusive—'Pappy' Noel Comes Through," and "First Photos from Korean POW Camp," and "Captured AP Lensman Scores Exclusive from behind Iron Curtain." Several newspapers ran full pages of Noel's photos. Swinton's prediction, happily, was 100 percent correct.

Noel and another prisoner later escaped from the camp, but they were captured three days later and sentenced to seven and one half weeks in solitary confinement on a reduced diet.

On March 28, 1953, the following letter from Frank Noel reached Al Resch in New York:

Dear Al,

I guess most everyone runs out of film now and then, and now it seems to be my turn. That is about the extent of my requirements, both personal and professional.

The next time you talk to Bob Schutz, tell him his camera is still perking like the movie popcorn toaster.

Other than for a couple of minor repairs, the outfit is still as good as it was when it was flung over the fence. I am very pleased that you and Alan Gould [executive editor of the AP] keep Evelyn [Mrs. Noel] posted whenever there is any news about me.

If you can get me some film packs, bulbs, and batteries, I'll be back in business....

Al, I am making a copy of this and send both, hoping that one will reach you. My health is first class and I'm darn sure getting plenty of rest. A vacation when I get out of here will just make me tired. I'm ready to pick up where I left off—anywhere you say....

Bossman, so-long for the time being. Be assured I am more than glad to keep cobwebs off the camera as long as you can still use the stuff.

Very warmest regards to the gang. Frank.

Noel made several hundred pictures in that camp that were serviced to American newspapers. He was released on August 9, 1953, after thirty-two months of imprisonment.

DAVID DOUGLAS DUNCAN

Perhaps the top photographer of the Korean conflict was David Douglas Duncan, who covered the war for *Life*. An ex-marine who had made spectacular combat photos in World War II, Duncan was the first American photographer on the scene in Korea when hostilities erupted. He was in Tokyo doing a photo-essay on Japanese art when the invasion came, and he was sent to the front at once. Two months later, he sent a telegram to the *Life* offices:

Trying to give you story which is timeless nameless dateless wordless which says very simply quietly this is war.

To get this story, Duncan made his way to the most forward unit of the First Marine Brigade—Company B of the Fifth Regiment—just as they began their push across the Naktong River. He carried his film in a backpack, along with a toothbrush, a bar of soap, a bottle of insect repellent, a blanket, a waterproof poncho, and an extra pair of socks.

His company was cut off from the main force. It was rapidly running out of ammunition. It had no radio contact with the other units. The desperate marines were oblivious to Duncan's camera. He photographed one

OPPOSITE: The most memorable photo of the Korean War was taken August 8, 1950 by Signal Corps photographer Sergeant Al Chang. A grief-stricken GI whose buddy was just killed is comforted by another infantryman during fighting in the Hoktong-Ni area.

BELOW: Marine Cpl. M.J. Bolhower took this shot of a recoilless rifle crew going into action against an enemy strongpoint somewhere near Chinchon-ni, Korea on April 16, 1951.

young marine with tears staining his face as he said over and over, "No men, no ammo, no nothing."

Duncan's pictures were published in September 1950, under the title: "This Is War." The editors at *Life* thought that the photos were so vivid that they ran them without captions.

A grimy sergeant, after seeing the pictures in *Life*, approached Duncan and said, "Geez, Dave, you don't make us look very pretty." Duncan laughed and said, "Are we?" The sergeant hesitated a moment, then said, "Well, I guess we ain't. And I guess the folks at home might as well know it."

Some time later, when twenty thousand men of the First Marine Division—Duncan's World War II unit—were surrounded in the Changjin reservoir area (where Frank Noel had been captured), Duncan talked a military pilot into landing him in their midst.

He wrote, "I want to give the reader something of the feeling of the guy under fire, his behavior in the presence of threatening death."

The temperature hovered between ten and thirty degrees below zero F (-23°–34°C). Duncan had to hold his camera next to his body to thaw the camera out each time he wanted to take pictures, and he had to wind the film slowly so that it would not snap in the brittle cold.

Many of his photos were close-ups of marines' faces. He observed, "Eyes of men who have looked on undiluted hell are not pleasant to meet....There is no fear in their faces and no great hatred."

> **Duncan was the first photographer to fly on a jet combat mission. Afterward, he telegraphed this message to New York, published in the 1951 *U.S. Camera Annual***

We were going over six hundred miles [960km] an hour but I didn't know it. The earth and sky, life and death, all that is and ever had been was crushing me lower toward the floor of the cockpit and showering thunderbolts over my head and shoulders and down along my spine. Sweat burst out all over my body, not as sweat usually is, but in rushing rivers which drenched my clothes, soaked the parachute and filled my eyes with burning tears. Then as the plane leveled off and the vise began to release me I managed to raise my head slightly and saw that glittering gems of canary-colored liquid were splashing down upon my knees and safety belt, where they lay shimmering. Others escaped through my clenched teeth and from my nose, and I thought to myself, "but these are priceless and very beautiful but should stay deep inside me, for they are what make me tick. Something secret must have broken and these are its melted parts." I wasn't ill, nor were these gems priceless. In its agony and protest my body had simply reacted within the limits of human limitation and had driven its juices back along my system.

Sweeping back over our home runway and in for the landing, I looked out at the raked-back wings with bulletlike tanks at their tips, then...at the little round stains on my knees which were dry and now without color, and I knew that for a short time I had actually been living in another world, a world which now lay beyond me and into which I would never set foot once that jet rolled to a stop in its place by the squadron shack.

And I was glad...Endit...Saludos...Duncan.

Photo historian Peter Pollock has this to say: "Duncan and his camera became to those marines what Ernie Pyle and his typewriter had been to the GIs of World War II."

CARL MYDANS

Life photographer Carl Mydans was in New York when the war broke out, but he rushed back to Tokyo immediately, where he had been assigned since the end of World War II. Ten days after the fighting started, he was in Korea headed for the front. He was dug in with the Thirty-fourth Infantry Regiment when the North Koreans launched an attack. The Americans held their own until the enemy brought in tanks. The GIs soon ran out of ammunition and retreated. As usual, Mydans was in the thick of it, covering the retreat, then following the Allied advances. His pictures enabled *Life* to score many "scoops."

In his 1959 book *More Than Meets The Eye*, Mydans recounts his thoughts on the day he left Korea:

Suddenly I felt a surge of gladness that I had been there, that I had seen it all and felt it all. And I was glad too, despite all I knew of men's inhumanity and brutality, to be a man, living among men. For I knew then, with that moment's insight, that this is my home, this world, this war-torn world. And this is my time and my place in it.

Each of us has a role, a time, a place. Those who are most fortunate discover what it is...

All of us live in history, whether we are aware of it or not, and die in drama. The sense of history and of drama comes to a man not because of who he is or what he does but flickeringly, as he is caught up in events, as his personality reacts, as he sees for a moment his place in the great flowing river of time and humanity...

I cannot tell you where our history is leading us, or through what suffering, or into what era of war or peace. But wherever it is, I know men of good heart will be passing there.

CHAPTER EIGHT

THE VIETNAM WAR

HORST FAAS COVERS THE MEKONG DELTA

"A lot of guys take chances in covering this dirty, shifting war, but the camera boys take the biggest chances and take them most often."

Time magazine, June 10, 1966

Shortly before World War II, the French protectorate of Vietnam was occupied by Japan as a base from which to invade Malaya. After the war, the Communist Party began to grow in popularity among the Vietnamese people. The French opposed the Communists' bid for power, and war broke out. In May 1954, French forces were decisively beaten at the battle of Dienbienphu. A cease-fire accord was signed, in which France agreed to divide the country along the Ben Hai River (12th parallel). Saigon was chosen as the capital of the Republic of Vietnam, and Hanoi was named the capital of the Democratic Republic of Vietnam. The two governments soon became embroiled in armed conflict, and the United States directly intervened on the side of Saigon. As the size of the American military commitment grew, the number of American combat photographers in Vietnam also grew.

HORST FAAS

Many observers—including the *New York Times* and *Time* magazine—have called Horst Faas the war's best photographer. In 1965, Faas became the first photographer to win both the Pulitzer Prize for news photography

OPPOSITE: This spectacular photo, hailed by David Douglas Duncan as the best of the Vietnam War, was taken by Associated Press photographer Art Greenspon in April 1968, and shows a GI guiding an evacuation helicopter into position to pick up casualties from a jungle offensive.

LEFT: Armed only with three Nikons, Associated Press photographer Horst Faas starts out on a jungle patrol in Vietnam.

and the Robert Capa Award of the Overseas Press Club in the same year.

Born in Berlin, Faas started his photographic career in 1952 with the Keystone Picture Agency in Berlin. In 1956, he joined the Berlin Associated Press bureau as a photographer assigned to the Bonn bureau.

His first experience in combat was in the Congo in 1960. Later, he went to Algeria and to Vietnam.

Dan DeLuce, assistant general manager of the AP, said of Faas,

> He's got on to the secret a long time ago that the human face is probably the most exciting piece of picture copy in the world. I can take any one of Horst's pictures and give you a closeup of a face and you don't have to see the rest of the scenery. The face is something by itself. It sells the pictures.

A Vietnamese general said that Horst Faas was "the luckiest man alive," just after Faas had emerged unscathed from a mission where men on all sides of him were cut down by Vietcong fire. In 1965, Faas was under mortar fire three times; he was twice with troops that were mistakenly bombed by friendly aircraft; he was caught in range of U.S. helicopter fire several times; he was once aboard a helicopter that crashed; three times he

photographed units that were wiped out shortly after he left them; and he was pinned down four times by machine-gun fire across rice paddies. Faas passes off his harrowing experiences as "unpleasantries." But he admits that several times he was unable to steady his hands to take a picture.

In June 1965, he suddenly found himself close enough to a Vietcong soldier to take a picture.

He was in Saigon when he got a report of a Communist attack near the town of Dongxoai, and he knew that government reinforcements would soon be going in. He put on his uniform, grabbed his camera equipment and steel helmet, jumped into his jeep, and hurried for the military airfield at Bien Hoa. Near the main gate of the field, his jeep had a flat tire. While he was changing it, he saw the first wave of ten helicopters take off.

"I was really miserable," he said, "because you have to go with the first wave into these relief operations. That's usually when things happen."

He finished fixing the tire and rushed to the pilot's room to wait for the choppers to return. When they began to arrive, he learned that two had been shot down and that all two hundred soldiers in the first wave had been caught in machine-gun and mortar fire and been killed within a few minutes. The second wave, too, was wiped out, but the third and fourth waves survived the initial landing. Faas went with the fifth wave.

Shortly after landing, he was told that the troops were about to retreat and that he was to be ready to move out. Just then, another helicopter came in carrying ammunition.

"I thought, 'Get on this helicopter. Get out and you'll definitely be alive the next morning.'" But he realized that the Vietcong would be shooting at it as it took off because it was exposed, so he did not get in. The craft took off and was hit immediately by heavy groundfire.

Many of the wounded inside were killed by bullets piercing the helicopter, and most of the occupants died. "The decision not to go aboard was based on experience," Faas said. Back on the ground, everything became confused. Many GIs were running, and Faas joined the retreat. After running a few yards, he looked across a road and saw what he thought was a "friendly" peering over the wall of a bunker, and he took his picture.

"This guy was surprised and I was surprised. He popped up twice and then nothing. A soldier pointed at me, laughed, and said, 'VC, VC.' I went around the corner. Two minutes later, a big bomb exploded in the bunker and I knew the guy must be dead by then. That's what makes a battle. It's all confusing."

Of the operation on June 11, 1965, Faas reported,

> Of some three hundred government troops that landed as reinforcements early yesterday morning, only three are left. These three lone Vietnamese survivors staggered out of the jungle early this morning. The rest, including three American advisors, are gone somewhere in the hell of Dongxoai. Two Americans also staggered out of the jungle, both wounded in the leg, clothed in rags and chattering incoherently in shock. They had been at the special forces camp a mile [1.6km] from Dongxoai that was smashed in the initial attack. Somehow they survived in the jungle.

For his own survival, Faas depended not only on his good luck, but also on his ability to detect a unit's fighting qualities. Before he would go into combat with an American or a Vietnamese battalion, he would look it over carefully. If he decided the unit's discipline was poor—that it would react poorly under fire—he would find another outfit.

Faas had some advice about narrowing the risks when taking photographs in combat:

> Never take pictures when the odds are against you. The most graphic picture I have ever seen was one I decided not to take because of a little added danger that might kill the careless. There were three dead American soldiers lying two hundred yards [180m] away—but I never got there because the area between them and me was under sniper fire.... The VC will shoot at anyone who stands out in the crowd, and correspondents in civilian garb are considered CIA agents by the Vietcong. When troops get into a fight, I go with them but since I carry no weapon and do not take part in the fighting, I keep my head down—the privilege of a non-combatant.

Another way to avoid getting killed, he said, was to stay away from men carrying radios with antennas visible because the VC tried to shoot radiomen first.

Faas was once asked if he thought he was brave. He answered very softly,

> No, no, no, no. Nobody's brave. That's a bad word. You get used to it. You learn. You learn. That's the only way. When bravery begins, then

stupidity begins too—especially in photography. When somebody thinks he has to take a picture, for any price, that's rather stupid. Going into Dongxoai was a great thing, but I wouldn't do it again. Even for fifteen or twenty pages in *Life*, I wouldn't do it again.

Once in combat, Faas' methods were simple.

You don't move your camera! You don't focus! You just look through it and—click! And click when things are moving. Don't click when people look at you and everything is static.

Because Faas was always in the thick of battle, he was valuable to the AP as a reporter. As soon as he returned from an engagement, other AP writers quickly debriefed him, writing stories based on what he had seen and giving him the byline. On March 21, 1965, for example, he rode with South Vietnamese troops on a helicopter expedition against Vietcong guerrillas.

The operation seemed somehow unusual to him, and he began asking questions. He came up with a story that American correspondents had been trying to pin down for months. The lead of the end product read: "United States and Vietnamese military forces are experimenting with nonlethal gas warfare in South Vietnam, highly reliable sources reported today."

Other AP photographers in Vietnam included Edward T. Adams, Al Chang, Henri Huet, Richard Merron, John Nance, John T. Wheeler, and Peter Arnett.

DAVID HUME KENNERLY

The man who became the best-known Vietnam photographer, David Hume Kennerly, won the 1972 Pulitzer Prize for Feature Photography for his war coverage. NBC made his autobiographical book, *Shooter*, into a television movie. The film and the book recount many of Kennerly's experiences as a Vietnam War photographer.

Kennerly credits David Douglas Duncan with giving him the best advice about how to survive in combat situations: "Stay with the old sarge." Kennerly followed the advice and always made it a point to stick close to the combat veterans. He also believes that surviving in combat is a matter of intelligence and common sense: "You can't be reckless and live to a ripe old age."

Kennerly later became the official White House photographer for President Gerald Ford.

HUYNH THANH MY

AP photographer Huynh Thanh My was born in the Mekong Delta. He was already covering the war for an

BELOW LEFT: Associated Press photographer Huynh Thanh My covers an action in Vietnam.

BELOW RIGHT: Matt Franjola took this picture of Pulitzer Prize-winner David Hume Kennerly in 1972 near Pleiku in Vietnam's central highlands.

American television company when he was spotted by Horst Faas and subsequently hired by AP.

My never refused an assignment. On May 27, 1965, for example, he was wounded and bleeding profusely, but he kept taking pictures until he could not work the shutter. Then he set his camera and gave it to a soldier who took more pictures of the battle, including a few of My. While covering a demonstration in Saigon, My was beaten by both rioters and police.

A few days before he was overthrown, former Vietnamese strongman Major General Nguyen Khanh said, "I like that man My's courage. I must see to it that he gets decorated for the work he is doing."

My was killed in action on October 13, 1965. He was given a posthumous award for valor in the Thirty-second Annual Headliners Club competition.

Horst Faas, who brought My to AP, said of his death:

When Huynh Thanh My died, he had done all the right things. He was with one of the best units. He stayed where the action was. He did not leave the assaulting unit and get lost in the rear. He was plainly unlucky. In a war without front lines, events can only be seen clearly and accurately when the reporter himself sees them happen, alongside the troops. To be there an hour later, or a few miles away, is to see a situation which often looks "back to normal." It would be impossible in this way to re-create in words or in photos what has happened and what it all meant to the soldiers and civilians involved. We have to report the facts at first-hand. I think we can only do so if we continue as we have, despite the tragic deaths.

KYOICHI SAWADA

Kyoichi Sawada was the first United Press International combat photographer to win a Pulitzer Prize. Born in 1936 in Aomori City in Japan, Sawada bought his first camera at age thirteen with money he had made delivering papers. He joined UPI in Tokyo in 1960 and was assigned to Vietnam in 1965.

In his first seven months in South Vietnam, he covered forty battles and campaigns. He learned to watch for certain clues that a major battle was in the offing. If a large group of soldiers was slated for a mission, for example, he would gamble that a major operation was underway, and he would get clearance to go along. He also kept an eye on the medical evacuation helicopters. "If a bunch of them are ready to take off," he said, "there's a big operation going on somewhere. You have to find out where, and try to tag along."

In December 1965, Sawada entered his combat photos in the Tenth Annual World Press Photo Exhibition at the Hague, the Netherlands. He won the grand prize. In 1966, he won both the Pulitzer Prize and an Overseas Press Club Award. Among the photographs in the portfolio that won him the Pulitzer was a picture entitled "Flee to Safety." It shows a Vietnamese family wading frantically across a river to escape the Vietcong.

JAMES PICKERELL

The first UPI photographer on the scene at the outbreak of the war was James Pickerell, now one of the most

OPPOSITE: A grieving father holds up the body of his child, killed during a battle on March 19, 1964, as Vietnamese Rangers look down from a tank. This picture was one of a series that won a Pulitzer Prize for Associated Press photographer Horst Faas.
BELOW: Wounded Private Thomas Cole, a medic from Richmond, Va., looks up with one unbandaged eye as he continues to tend other wounded men during a firefight between U.S. First Air Cavalry units and enemy troops. This photo was taken in January 1966 by Associated Press photographer Henri Huet. A month later Huet was killed in action in a helicopter crash in Laos.

This Horst Faas photo shows Vietnamese commandos being dropped from helicopters onto a graveyard near the Delta town of Mo Cay on Nov. 4, 1964.

widely published photographers of the war. Pickerell went to Asia after graduating from UCLA; he had been to Asia earlier as a navy photographer and decided to go back as a freelancer. He was in Tokyo when the conflict heated up, and UPI offered him a job and transportation to Saigon if he would cover the war. He arrived in the middle of a Buddhist demonstration against the government of President Ngo Dinh Diem and shot twenty-five rolls of film. His first photo made the cover of *Life*. A friend said wryly, "What a way to start a career—first story shot makes *Life*."

As the war grew and shifted to the swamps and mountain jungles, Pickerell followed the troops. He usually carried five camera bodies.

Some photographers carry much less than I do, yet when the shooting starts, you want to have the right camera, the right lens and the right film ready. If you don't, you'll miss the story and I can't take the chance.

On one occasion, Pickerell was moving along a canal with a Vietnamese Ranger outfit. There was no sign of the enemy, so he moved ahead of the troops to get a picture of the Rangers advancing. He took the picture, then looked behind him to see a Vietcong guerrilla. The VC soldier took aim, and Pickerell hit the dirt trying to find cover. Shots rang out, and Pickerell felt a hot numbness in his leg, making him the first American correspondent wounded in action there.

A Vietnamese medic rushed to him and bandaged up the .30 caliber bullet hole in his leg. The American army advisor called in a medical evacuation helicopter, and within ten minutes Pickerell was on his way to Tan Son Nhut airbase at Saigon where he would be transferred to a military hospital.

While he was recuperating, the American advisors were becoming soldiers and fighting the Vietcong themselves. Pickerell decided he would be better off as a freelancer again, so he made arrangements with the Black Star Agency to handle his photos. He was soon back at the front, and in September 1964, his first *Newsweek* cover appeared. The next year, five more appeared.

Pickerell had a knack for sensing where the fighting would be. For example, in early 1966 he was with the marines near Danang when an operation was being read-

This photo of an American GI walking over a battle-scarred hill in Vietnam was one of a series that won the Pulitzer Prize for United Press International photographer David Hume Kennerly.

ied. He had a choice of joining any of three companies. He noticed the battle plan called for the Second Company to move through some villages and decided that this held the best chance for action. His hunch paid off: as the marines approached one village, they drew sniper fire and returned it with grenades and rifle fire. As the marines charged through the village, Pickerell photographed a weeping woman clutching her child in terror, her hut burning in the background, while a marine tried to comfort her.

The picture ran full-page in *Newsweek* and was featured in many other publications. The photo dramatized the central tragedy of the war—the plight of civilians caught in the horror of guerrilla warfare.

On another occasion, Pickerell was advancing with Vietnamese troops through territory thought to be infested with Vietcong. Some sniper fire cracked through the trees, and the Vietnamese troops returned the fire, then moved into a nearby village, which they burned. A villager flushed out of hiding was interrogated, and Pickerell shot a few pictures. He had just looked away for other pictures to take when he heard the Vietnamese officer say to an American officer, "I think I'll shoot this man." Pickerell turned just as the Vietnamese raised his carbine and shot the prisoner through the head. The picture was blurred, but it captured the brutality of the execution. He took other pictures on that spot, and the sequence was published over nine pages in the London *Weekend Telegraph*.

DICKEY CHAPELLE

Dickey Chapelle of the *National Observer* was the first American woman combat photographer to be killed in action.

Chapelle was born in Milwaukee in 1919. Intent on being an airplane designer, she entered Massachusetts Institute of Technology on a scholarship. But a year later, at the beginning of World War II, she left school and went to New York City to learn more about her newest interest—photography.

She was hired by *Woman's Day* magazine to photograph the war from a woman's angle. In the South Pacific, she snapped a picture entitled "The Dying Marine." The marine's life was saved, however, through the use of blood plasma, and the Red Cross used the picture in a nationwide blood drive.

After the war, she worked for a time as a magazine photographer in New York City. She then volunteered to work for the American Friends Service Committee to photograph the Friends' relief activities in Europe. In 1952, she parachuted into Korea with the U.S. Special Forces. In November 1956, she returned to Europe to photograph the escapee movement across the Iron Curtain. She was captured by the Communists in Hungary while on the assignment and was imprisoned for fifty days. Later, she spent several months in the field with Algerian rebel forces. She went into Lebanon with the U.S. Marines. In June 1965,

A dead American GI lies in the foreground as soldiers advance on a hill near the town of Cholon in this photo by Kyoichi Sawada.

she flew to Santo Domingo to cover the fighting in the Dominican Republic, where she infiltrated rebel lines to photograph one of their commanders.

Vietnam was the fourth war she had covered. She was over forty years old, but she jumped with paratroopers and was the only American combat photographer fully accredited as a paratrooper by both the American and the Vietnamese armed forces. On her five trips to Vietnam she covered eleven major campaigns. She died while photographing five marines on patrol near Danang. A Marine a few steps in front of her stepped on a hidden booby-trap wire, and she was hit in the neck with shrapnel. She was dead before the aid station could be reached. She was forty-six.

Her last telegram to the *National Observer*, dated October 18, 1965, shows what she was thinking and doing in Vietnam:

Tomorrow I leave here for Danang. I'll try to begin doing the coverage of the marines there by riding on the star mission of their logistics—huge tanker planes commuting from El Toro via Okinawa which refuel aloft the jet fighter planes covering marine actions on the ground. It is aboard these same planes that I've made most of my own Pacific crossings, the Honolulu–Manila lap, so I can write about them firsthand. However, should the pace of ground operations against the Vietcong pick up again—it seems to be in a lull right now—of course I'll go out on the ground first, and do the logistic bit after or between covering the ground fighting.

National Observer executive William Giles tried to explain the respect American soldiers felt for Chapelle:

I do not know how the mutual romance and respect between Dickey Chapelle from Milwaukee and the American fighting man first began or what impelled her to travel all over this globe to be where he was and take part in what he was doing. I just know that it was genuine—aboard the hospital ship anchored off Iwo Jima, in the muck of Korea, in the jungles of Vietnam. She was there by choice, and aggressive, insistent choice. Perhaps she had to be because, basically, she was a news reporter covering what she knew to be the most compelling news story of our time.

It was also said of her, "She shared the terrors, the privations,...and the triumphs. And more, she understood them. She had the ability to convey the reality of war to film and paper in a degree seldom matched."

After her death, she was cited with a special mention award by the Overseas Press Club. The judges said,

Rarely have daring, integrity, efficiency and human warmth been as perfectly matched as in our friend and colleague, Dickey Chapelle. She deserves a separate tribute all her own.

Her only book, *What's a Woman Doing Here?* which was published in 1961, states:

This is the story I have been writing, episode by episode, for twenty years: the story of

**OPPOSITE: Kyoichi Sawada took this picture of two South Vietnamese carrying a wounded relative.
BELOW: Terrified children flee after a napalm strike. This picture, taken by Huyng Cong "Nick" Ut, won the AP Managing Editor's Best Photo Award.**

One of the many outstanding U.S. navy photographers to cover Vietnam was Jean C. Cote, who took this picture showing a Vietcong suspect guarded by a marine while other marines search the beach at Vung Mu.

men brave enough to risk their lives in the defense of freedom against tyranny. To me it has always been the most important story in the world.

Many other photographers were killed in Vietnam. *Life* magazine's outstanding photographer Larry Burrows, who won the 1966 Robert Capa Award for his picture story entitled "With a Brave Crew on a Deadly Flight," died in a helicopter crash in 1971.

ROBERT CAPA

Yet another *Life* photographer killed was Robert Capa. His last mission is described by correspondent John Mecklinin the Epilogue to Capa's *Images of War*.

In the bug-ridden room of a Nam Dinh establishment which calls itself the Modern Hotel, Bob Capa sucked a glass of warm cognac and soda and made a pronouncement: "This is

A South Vietnamese woman cries over the body of her child in this picture from Horst Faas's Pulitzer Prize-winning portfolio. The picture also won the 1970 Sigma Delta Chi award.

Dana Stone took this picture of South Vietnamese civilians looking for relatives among the bodies of Da Nang residents killed by terrorists.

maybe the last good war. The trouble with all you guys who complain so much about the French public relations is that you don't appreciate this is a reporter's war. Nobody knows anything and nobody tells you anything, and that means a good reporter is free to go out and get a beat every day."

Capa and I had been touring French outposts in the besieged Red River Delta with General Rene Cogny, French commander in northern Vietnam.

Next day we were going out with a two-thousand-man task force which was to relieve, then evacuate, two garrisons some fifty miles [80km] south of Hanoi....

When the jeep appeared at 7 A.M. May 25 [1954], we climbed in along with Scripps-Howard Correspondent Jim Lucas. Waiting for the Red River ferry just outside Nam Dinh, Capa announced, "This is going to be a beautiful story. I shall be on my good behavior today. I shall not insult people and I shall not even mention the excellence of my work."

On his delta tour Capa had got the idea of a picture story to be entitled "Bitter Rice." His plan was to dramatize the contrast of tanks next to peasants working in the paddies, of men dying in the struggle for the rice harvest.

All morning he worked to photograph peasants carrying rice to market in straw baskets,

plodding along the edges of vehicle-clogged roads....

"We heard that French Union elements had reached Doai Than, the first of two posts the column was to relieve. We got there in about ten minutes, arriving at 2:25 P.M. Capa wanted to press on, saying "The story's almost done, but I need the fort blowing up."

The sun beat down fiercely. There was fire in every direction: French artillery, tanks and mortars behind us, the chatter of small arms from the woods surrounding a village 500 yards [450m] to our left, heavy small-arms fire mixed with exploding French shells in another village 500 yards ahead and to our right, the sporadic ping of slugs passing overhead, the harrowing curr-rump of mines and enemy mortars....

Capa was exquisitely bored and climbed up on the road, saying, "I'm going up the road a little bit. Look for me when you get started again....

A few minutes later a tank began firing right behind us. The French were mortaring the village to our left and at 3:05 Moroccan infantrymen began advancing through the paddies to finish the job. I was making notes of this when a helmeted soldier arrived and spoke to the lieutenant in Vietnamese.

Without a trace of emotion the lieutenant said, *"Le photographe est mort."* I understood

A tank rumbles past bodies of South Vietnamese civilians killed in Da Nang in a Vietcong attack.

OPPOSITE: Many of the great Vietnam War photos were taken by U.S. navy photographers trained in a special program at Syracuse University. This photo, taken by PHC C.S. Dodd, shows navy personnel providing security for an Army Medical Evacuation helicopter picking up wounded along the Van Co Tay River in 1964.

the words but they didn't register and I said, "Pardon?" The lieutenant repeated the sentence in the same flat voice. This time the words registered, but I was certain I had misunderstood and said to Lucas almost as a joke, "This guy's trying to tell me Capa's dead...."

A second Vietnamese ran up and beckoned directly to me. The lieutenant questioned him and relayed, "Maybe not dead but wounded by mortar, *très grave*."

Lucas and I jumped up and ran with the soldier down the ditch. At the point where the road bent soldiers pointed up and over the road, then disappeared. We scrambled across the road into a small lowland field. At the foot of the dike across the V formed by the bending road Capa lay on his back, the stump of his shattered left leg about a foot [30cm] from a hole blown in the earth by the explosion. He also had a grievous chest wound. One camera was clutched in his left hand. I began calling his name. The second or third time his lips moved slightly like those of a man disturbed in a sleep. That was his last movement. It was 3:10 P.M.

At Nam Dinh, where the casket was loaded aboard a C-47 for shipment to Hanoi, Zone Commander Colonel Paul Vanuxen turned out a Senegalese honor guard. In Saigon General Navarre sent condolences to the United States embassy. In Hanoi, where the body was taken to the French cemetery for temporary burial, General Cogny ordered an honor guard of nineteen red-bereted colonial paratroopers and sent a large wreath. There was also a wreath from the army's press information service and a third wreath inscribed *A notre ami.*

At the cemetery, General Cogny, impeccable in full dress uniform, stood stiffly at salute for a full minute before the casket. He then turned to the assembled newsmen and delivered a brief but emotional speech. Capa, he said, "fell as a soldier among soldiers." He then bent down and pinned a medal on the American flag that was draped over the casket. It was one of France's highest military honors: Croix de Guerre with Palm, Order of the Army.

John Steinbeck, who knew Capa in World War II and later accompanied him to Russia, had this to say about the effectiveness of Capa's photographs:

Capa's pictures were made in his brain, the camera only completed them. You can no more mistake his work than you can the canvas of a fine painter. Capa knew what to look for and what to do with it when he found it. His camera caught and held emotion. Capa's work is itself the picture of a great heart and overwhelming passion.

Military photographers provided the armed forces with intensive coverage of the Vietnam War. Signal Corps photographers were assigned to the war in one of two ways.

First, each division assigned a photographer to cover the public information and documentary function for that organization. Second, specific assignments for the army were made through the U.S. Special Photographic Detachment, Pacific, based in Hawaii. One officer said, "These men are free to accomplish their mission—no one bothers them with hometown release pictures or officers' club assignments."

The tragedy of the Vietnam War did not stop new talent from emerging or new reputations from being made. In fact, it is precisely in the midst of tragedy that a good photographer can find some of the most poignant subjects for his camera.

Dick Halstead, who headed UPI's photo operation in Vietnam and who took many photos there himself, puts it this way,

There's a tendency in the States for a young guy who wants to break into editorial photography to feel there's a closed shop against him—until somehow he gets a reputation. He can get an instant reputation here [in Vietnam]. He has to provide his own means of getting here, but if he can take pictures, we'll help him get his accreditations; we'll give him film; we'll take care of all his processing; we'll pay him fifteen bucks, cash on the line, for each picture we send out; and we'll send it with his credit line. There's no premium—right now, anyway—on length of service, background, experience, or whatever they call it. There's no background for combat photography anyway. It's different. In this war, it takes initiative and guts—and mostly initiative.

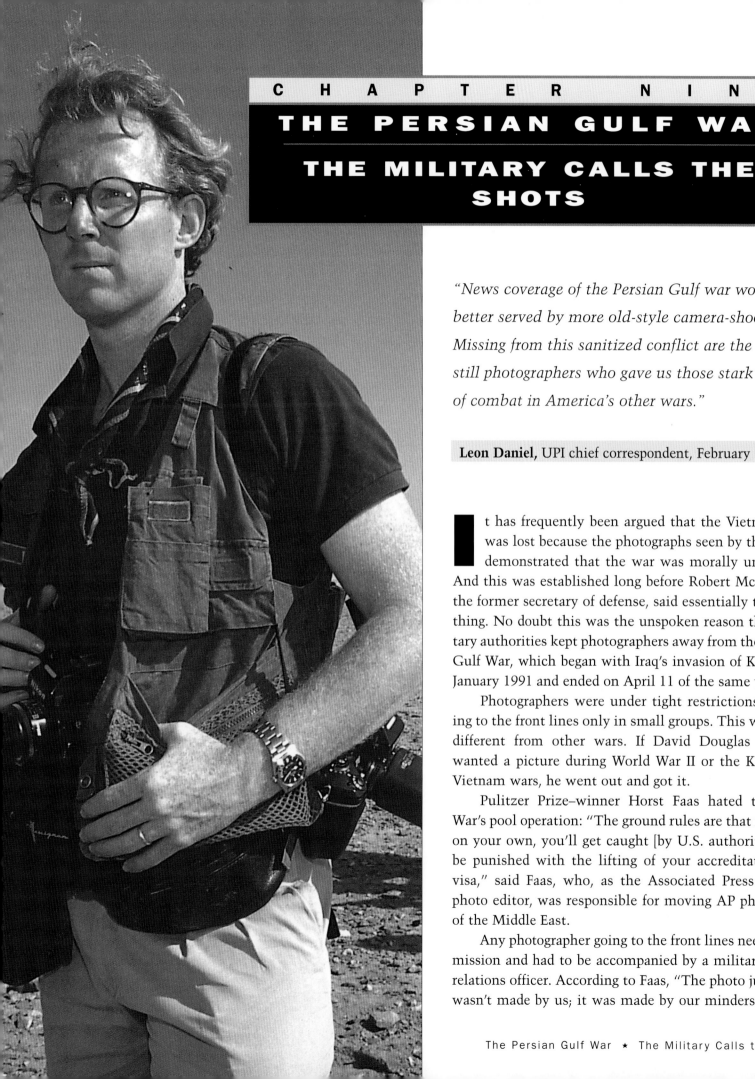

CHAPTER NINE

THE PERSIAN GULF WAR

THE MILITARY CALLS THE SHOTS

"News coverage of the Persian Gulf war would be better served by more old-style camera-shooters. Missing from this sanitized conflict are the great still photographers who gave us those stark images of combat in America's other wars."

Leon Daniel, UPI chief correspondent, February 12, 1991

It has frequently been argued that the Vietnam War was lost because the photographs seen by the public demonstrated that the war was morally untenable. And this was established long before Robert McNamara, the former secretary of defense, said essentially the same thing. No doubt this was the unspoken reason that military authorities kept photographers away from the Persian Gulf War, which began with Iraq's invasion of Kuwait in January 1991 and ended on April 11 of the same year.

Photographers were under tight restrictions, traveling to the front lines only in small groups. This was quite different from other wars. If David Douglas Duncan wanted a picture during World War II or the Korean or Vietnam wars, he went out and got it.

Pulitzer Prize–winner Horst Faas hated the Gulf War's pool operation: "The ground rules are that if you go on your own, you'll get caught [by U.S. authorities] and be punished with the lifting of your accreditation and visa," said Faas, who, as the Associated Press London photo editor, was responsible for moving AP photos out of the Middle East.

Any photographer going to the front lines needed permission and had to be accompanied by a military public relations officer. According to Faas, "The photo judgment wasn't made by us; it was made by our minders. We did

OPPOSITE: Reuter photographer Will Burgess took this dramatic shot of an Iraqi tank sillhouetted against an oil well fire at the Burgan oil field near Kuwait City.
LEFT: David Turnley, working in the Persian Gulf for the Black Star agency, managed to take some impressive shots despite the military's strict controls.

not see any wounded; we did not see any dead." He thinks photographers should be allowed to risk their own lives with the soldiers. He says that journalists can understand and observe simple rules of security and wouldn't jeopardize any military operation. "Of course nobody in the right sense of mind writes about operations that are planned, or how many tanks are moving," he says. "On the other hand, what is it worth if a briefing officer tells you ten days later that these marines were killed by friendly fire?" He believes that photographs taken at the scene of the fighting would have humanized the Gulf War.

The debate raged in press circles over whether pictures of wounded and dead soldiers should even be declassified. Gary Fong, director of photography at the *San Francisco Chronicle*, said, "I think people are shocked to see a photo of an American soldier killed. I think the war is shocking enough without increasing the shock and bringing it right down to the breakfast table. I would tend to move away from that shocking image, especially of a GI."

On the other hand, former *Life* editor Philip Kunhardt has dealt with photographs of dying U.S. soldiers before, during the Vietnam years. He told Gannett

News Service, "If those kinds of pictures ever come out of this war—and who knows if they're going to, with all the control the government is imposing—there will be an enormous rush by the news magazines to put on very, very tough pictures."

Early in the war, *USA Today* carried a color photo of a bloodied Israeli victim of a Scud missile attack. It generated scores of protest calls. Newspaper and magazine editors are justifiably wary of upsetting their readers, but that caution is balanced by the need to tell the story.

The strict censorship prompted UPI's Chief Correspondent, Leon Daniel, writing out of Dhahran, Saudi Arabia, on February 12, 1991, to say, "Unless things change, the photographic legacy of this war is likely to be a lot of slick footage that looks like a video game, or shots of a general snipping a ribbon at a new mess hall."

In rebuttal, Department of Defense spokesman Pete Williams defended the limited access that photographers had to the desert battlefield, saying the Gulf War was unlike other wars, where photographers had more freedom. He said that of the fourteen hundred journalists and technicians in Saudi Arabia, only 192 were assigned to be with combat forces. "If a ground war begins on the Arabian Peninsula, the battlefield will be chaotic and the action will be violent. This will be modern, intense warfare," he said. There were too many journalists and photographers in Saudi Arabia, he said, to allow the military to say, "Y'all come to the battlefield."

Nonetheless, a few photographers managed to make remarkable photos during the war. One photographer, Sophie Ristelhueber, who had previously covered the skirmishes in Beirut, took pictures that range from the aerial, abstracted view, down to the details of the debris on the ground. Her Kuwait photographs were published in a book titled *Aftermath*, and an exhibition of her Gulf pictures was mounted at the Imperial War Museum in London.

OPPOSITE: U.S. marines play volleyball as a CH-53 transport helicopter takes off in the eastern Saudi desert. BELOW: An American GI walks past bodies of Iraqi soldiers near Basra as Kuwaiti oil wells burn in the background. Photo by Andy Clark.

Despite the regulations and precautions, a number of journalists were captured by Iraqis during the war. On March 4, 1991, a convoy of eight cars containing journalists—including photographers Philippe Wojazer and Santiago Lyon of Reuters and Todd Buchanan of the *Philadelphia Inquirer*—was taken prisoner at an Iraqi army checkpoint near Basra. They were released five days later.

Pictures taken by pool photographers were developed and printed by the Associated Press in Dhahran. After being censored by the military, the photos were screened by AP, Reuters, *Newsweek* and *Time*.

In an interview in *Views* magazine, *Boston Globe* photographer Jonathan Wiggs said,

> There were guidelines as to what you could show and not show. You could only state your dateline very generally: "somewhere in eastern

Saudi Arabia," for instance. We were not allowed to show dead Americans or the tower at Dhahran airport, for example. Well, OK, they didn't want landmarks. I had no problem with that but I strongly disagreed with the restrictions on photographing dead Americans. How could the U.S. government military tell its citizens how to do their job? It gets tricky, because you didn't want to do something that was going to endanger soldiers' lives. But certainly, if there are some dead Americans in a burned-out tank, and you take a photograph of it, I don't see how that's a danger to someone's life. That would simply demonstrate the real cruelty and finality of war to the American people. Clearly, they didn't want the public back home to see this side of the war.

As would be expected, the Associated Press needed a large number of photographers to cover the war and, at the same time, be of service to newspaper photographers. AP asked photographers from their worldwide bureaus to volunteer. Among those who did were John Gaps III, David Longstreath, Doug Mills, Scott Applewhite, Tanen Maury, Greg Gibson, Roberto Borea, Bob Jordan, Dave Martin, Laurent Rebours, Heribert Proepper, Peter DeJong, Sadayuki Mikami, Diether Endicher, Dominique Mollard, Greg English, and Michel Lipchitz.

OPPOSITE: Mike Marucci took this picture of a sailor manning a machine gun on the command ship *LaSalle*.
BELOW: Marines duck incoming fire in the town of Khafji. Picture by Charles Platiau.

OPPOSITE: An army
machine gun crew
is oblivious to the
Bedouin leading
his camel near the
Eighteenth Artillery
Corps camp in north-
eastern Saudi Arabia
on November 15,
1990, in this photo
taken by Frederic
Neema.

Among the Reuters photographers in the Gulf were Pat Benic, Santiago Lyon, Philippe Wojazer, Charles Platiau, William McNamee, and Richard Ellis.

Fifty U.S. Army photographers of the Combat Pictorial Detachment of the Eighteenth Airborne were stationed in the Gulf. Most of them used Nikon F4 cameras but, in order to speed transmission, a few used the Sony Still Video (NVC5000) camera. This was essentially an analog computer that was capable of recording images on a magnetic floppy disk. This camera made it quick and easy to transmit photos to the Pentagon, but the quality of the final product was not very good. (The army has since replaced its analog equipment with digital cameras made by Nikon.)

Detroit Free Press photographer David Turnley, working for the Black Star agency, took one of the most emotionally charged pictures to come out of the Gulf War, showing a soldier crying beside a helicopter with his buddy in a body bag.

Its photographic coverage of the Gulf War earned the army's Forty-ninth Public Affairs Detachment the Meritorious Unit Citation—an award usually reserved for larger units. Photographer Specialist Michael Hawn was awarded the Air Medal, and Major Michael Edrington, commander of the Fifty-fifth Signal company, received the Meritorious Service Medal and the Army Commendation Medal. Sergeant Raymond Roman received the Bronze Star for coverage of the Iraqi invasion.

The navy was driven to implement the electronic darkroom because of the demands of the Gulf War, according to Russ Egner of the navy's News Photo Division. Using the Nikon Digital Still Video camera, navy photographers could send images from any of nine aircraft carriers that were equipped with electronic dark-rooms. The images would be received in the Pentagon about forty minutes later; however, because of satellite availability, transmissions could only be sent between one and four in the morning, Egner said.

Forty-one marine combat cameramen served in the Gulf in detachments commanded by Captain Martha Conway, CWO Robert Adao, and CWO Charles Grow. The most heavily decorated was Lance Corporal Richard Price, who was awarded the Navy Commendation Medal with Combat V for valor. Other decorated marine photographers were Master Sergeant Mike Ortiz, Corporal Matthew Crabtree, and Lance Corporal Jimmy Johnson.

EPILOGUE
THAT'S HOW IT WAS

Over the 130 years in which thousands of Americans have taken millions of photographs to document American wars for posterity, the art of combat photography has changed considerably. Equipment, training, and time needed to have a photo published are quite different now.

Brady's Civil War photographers would set up their 6 by 8-inch [15.2 by 20.3cm] or 8 by 10-inch [20.3 by 25.4cm], or sometimes 11 by 14-inch [27.9 by 35.6] cameras on tripods, dash into the horse-drawn van, coat the wet collodion plate, run back to the camera, make the exposure of the scene, hurry back to the wagon, develop the plate, and then get behind the lines as quickly as possible without breaking any of the glass plates. Because the shortest possible exposure for the shorter lens was about three seconds—the longer lenses needed about twenty seconds, depending on the light—instantaneous views were impossible. The photographers were forced to wait for a quiet moment or to arrange groups to convey the impression of a candid snapshot. Subject matter was mostly limited to the dead of battle, buildings left standing, and landmarks of the battlefield. But when one considers the slow shutters and the shallow depth of field, it is amazing how favorably many Civil War photos compare to those taken in later wars.

By contrast, today's combat photographer has access to a huge range of cameras and lenses. The favorite camera is what used to be called a miniature camera—the 35mm, which features fast lenses and color film that can be pushed to 3,200 ASA. And many photographers in the Persian Gulf War used still video cameras, which allowed easy and quick transmission.

Early war photographers were self-taught or had been apprenticed to professional photographers. Most of their experience had been with studio situations with a constant light source, as opposed to outdoors where the light—and exposure—was constantly changing. By 1917, the military had realized the importance of combat photography, and the Signal Corps was given the responsibility of training photographers. An aerial photography school was started at Cornell University early in World War I.

More military photography schools were quickly established. Before the war ended, four thousand Signal Corps photographers had been trained at Columbia University in New York, and twenty-five hundred had studied aerial photography at Kodak Park in Rochester, New York.

Today, the majority of civilian and military photographers have attended college, and all branches of the armed forces have set up excellent photography schools.

But two aspects of war photography have remained constant over the years: danger from the enemy, and controversy over the use of certain photos. Will the photo that the combat photographer has just taken aid or hinder the war effort? Edward Steichen, at the end of World War I, regretted his role as a photographer.

By World War II, however, he had come to the conclusion that combat photos could serve as "a great deterrent of war. Pictures taken during the Civil War at the Andersonville, Georgia, Confederate prison were published extensively throughout the North. Jefferson Davis charged that, although these pictures were genuine, they were misleading, misrepresentative, and wrongly used. Pictures of prisoners taken by Confederate photographers

OPPOSITE: Twenty of the Marine Corps 4th Division photographers who covered the Iwo Jima invasion pose for Sgt. Morejohn with a captured Japanese battle flag during a lull in the fighting.

OPPOSITE: One of
the great human
interest photographs
of the Vietnam War
shows an anguished
navy corpsman,
himself caught in a
crossfire from North
Vietnamese machine
guns near the
Laotian border,
telling comrades,
"He's dead!" after
his efforts to save
a soldier failed.

were sent to Washington, but these were not published. Davis later wrote, "At the insistence of the Northerners, and against the judgment of our own surgeons, some of the worst cases were released." When the prisoners reached Annapolis, Davis charged, these indescribable wrecks of humanity were photographed as "specimen prisoners."

Some historians charge that the "yellow journals" were responsible for the Spanish-American War; it is a fact that editors throughout the country clamored for pictures of every encounter. Cecil Carnes, in writing about photographer Jimmy Hare, said:

> He snapped the wreck of the *Maine* from every point of the compass. He caught divers still busy at the somber task of bringing up the drowned. Jimmy prowled through concentration camps. He photographed swollen bodies with bones breaking through the skin; he took pictures of the emaciated living, and of babies ravaged with disease. Every ship that passed Morro Castle en route to New York carried a packet of snapshots. Their influence upon public opinion can hardly be overestimated.

In 1937, the *Des Moines Register and Tribune* ran an article on World War I pictures, entitled "War Propaganda Exposed." This article showed pictures released by Allied forces side by side with the counterpropaganda pictures of the Central Powers. Sketches of German soldiers killing and mutilating French and Belgian children were contrasted with photos—made by German photographers—that showed German soldiers treating French and Belgian children with utmost kindness. Pictures purporting to show German atrocities were branded as fakes by friend and foe alike.

Relatively few combat pictures are faked, but certain photographs can be used to advance the purposes of one group or another.

Joe Rosenthal's Iwo Jima flag-raising picture was called "one of the greatest propaganda pictures of all time" by Clifford Edom of the University of Missouri. Its publication was a positive force in America's effort to boost morale. And Dickey Chapelle's "Dying Marine" photo served as a great help to the Red Cross' blood-donation campaign.

The July 23, 1966, issue of *Editor & Publisher* reports a speech about Vietnam photography by General Paul D. Adams of the United States Strike Command, given to an audience of professional photographers. The general praised the photographer who took the picture of a young American medic, his head swathed in bandages, giving medical attention to other wounded soldiers. However, in a picture of a wounded Vietnamese woman and crying child, General Adams saw "an attempt to arrange American sympathies by and for one Vietnamese political faction against another." Editors obviously thought both pictures were newsworthy, so they were published.

But propaganda is in the eye of the beholder. Some people, depending on their political persuasion, might impute ulterior motives to the publication of any photograph. One person's "documentary" photo is another's "propaganda" photo.

Combat photographers should realize their obligation to objectivity and fairness and should photograph as many situations as possible, allowing their editor or photo officer to decide which "situation" to disseminate on the basis of impartial judgment.

The controversy over propaganda versus objective reporting has led to what many photojournalists view as anathema: censorship. Under the guise of protecting the photographers from danger, the American military has followed the lead of totalitarian governments and has prevented the free dissemination of information. Ironically, thanks to the thousands of military-trained photographers, every aspect of American wars are photographed. However, the American public may never see the most graphic war pictures.

In addition to the armed forces' contribution to documenting wars, a civilian organization stands out. In its heyday, *Life* magazine spared no expense to ensure that the American public knew what their servicemen were going through. And history will not forget the contribution of *Life* photographers such as Robert Capa, Larry Burrows, David Douglas Duncan, George Silk, W. Eugene Smith, Carl Mydans, and John Olson.

Robert Capa, who believed that he was engaged in a lofty and lasting effort—the pursuit of truth—gave war photographers something to live by when he stated that in years to come, former soldiers will look at his pictures of them in combat and say, "That's how it was."

GREAT PHOTOGRAPHERS OF AMERICAN WARS

EDWARD T. ADAMS

Born in 1933 in New Kensington, Pennsylvania. Joined the marines and was sent to Korea where he covered several engagements, as well as the prisoner of war exchange of 1953. After the war he worked for various newspapers, including the *Philadelphia Bulletin*. He later joined the Associated Press and was assigned to cover the Vietnam War. His Vietnam combat photos won the only awards given to an American in the 1964 World Press Photo Contest at The Hague—one for news photography and one in the feature category. After the war he became a freelance photographer in New York City.

PETER ARNETT

Born in Riverton, New Zealand, in 1934. He started his newspaper career in 1951 at Invercargill, New Zealand, and three years later went to Australia to work on the *Sydney Sun*. He left Australia in 1958 to work at the *Bangkok World* until 1960. He then joined the Associated Press, working in Laos, and later in Jakarta, Indonesia until 1962, when he was sent to Vietnam. There, he combined writing with photography and, in 1966, won the Pulitzer Prize for International Reporting. The magazine *AP World* said, "Many Arnett fans had fully expected him to be cited for his photography, too, since some of the most notable newsphotos from the Vietnam war-front have been his. As Arnett follows the troops with pad and pencil there's always a camera dangling in his chest....Somehow newsman Peter Arnett and photographer Horst Faas are linked together in reputation as the men most likely to get there fastest with the mostest in Vietnam."

OTIS AULTMAN

Born in Holden, Missouri, in 1876, he was the major photographer covering Pancho Villa and the Mexican Revolution that began in 1910. When the Mexicans raided the border town of Columbus, New Mexico in 1910, he took the first pictures that told the world about the atrocities committed there. Later he photographd General John Pershing's futile pursuit of Villa. He went on to work for the *El Paso Times*. He died March 6, 1943.

GEORGE N. BARNARD

Born on December 23, 1819 in Connecticut, Barnard was brought up in Nashville, Tennessee. He was a pioneer in the field of photography, starting to work as a "daguerrean artist" in 1843, only three years after Daguerre made public his photographic process. During the 1840s and 1850s, he worked in Oswego, New York and Syracuse, New York. An active and adventurous photographer, he took some of the earliest action news photos. When the Civil War broke out,

Barnard moved to Washington and, in the employ of Mathew Brady, documented Union armies, camps, and fortifications. In 1863 Barnard left Brady to work for Alexander Gardner. Immediately after the war, Barnard retraced the route of Sherman's march, making a series of photos which he published in 1864 under the title *Photographic Views of Sherman's Campaign*.

FELIX A. BEATO

Felix Beato was apparently born in Venice. He assisted the English photographer James Robertson at Constantinople in 1850, and together they photographed cities around the Mediterranean. Robertson documented the Crimean War in 1855, arriving there after Roger Fenton had left. Beato moved to Yokohama, Japan in the 1860s. In 1871, Beato was hired to photograph the unsuccessful mission to open Korea to the West by an American fleet under the command of Admiral Rogers. In the 1880s he photographed British troops at war in Egypt and in the Sudan.

MARGARET BOURKE-WHITE

Born in New York City in 1904, Margaret Bourke-White became interested in photography after taking a course in the subject at Columbia University. Her work attracted the attention of publisher Henry Luce who asked her to join his magazine *Fortune*. When *Life* made its debut in 1936, her picture of the Fort Peck Dam graced the cover. She was in the midst of battle from the very beginning of World War II, when the ship she was taking to cover the North African campaign was torpedoed and sunk. She spent two years covering the war on the Italian peninsula and was the only non-Russian and non-German photographer covering the siege of Moscow. Later, she photographed Germany's bombed-out cities and concentration camps. Her books include *You Have Seen Their Faces* with Erskine Caldwell; *North of the Danube* with Erskine Caldwell; *Shooting the Russian War*; *Purple Heart Valley*; *Dear Fatherland, Rest Quietly*; *Halfway to Freedom*; and *Portrait of Myself*.

MATHEW B. BRADY

Mathew Brady was born on a farm near Lake George, New York in 1882. He studied painting with William Page, who introduced him to Samuel F.B. Morse. He became a daguerreotypist in New York City around 1844. In 1858 he opened a studio in Washington, D.C., the Brady National Photographic Art Gallery. During the first year of the Civil War, Alexander Gardner, Timothy O'Sullivan, James Gibson, and other photographers worked for Brady. Their efforts provided some of the most coherent photographic coverage of the war. In 1869, Brady published *National Photographic Collection of War Views and Portraits of Representative Men* which included seven hundred scenes of battle areas and more than twenty-five hundred portraits. After the war Brady gradually lost his New York and Washington galleries to creditors, and at the end of his career was working as a

camera operator in galleries owned by others. He died in a charity hospital in New York in 1896.

GEORGE BURNS

George Burns grew up in Albany, New York, and worked as a staff photographer for the General Electric Company and the *Albany Times Union*. When World War II broke out he joined the army and then the staff of *Yank*. Burns photographed in the South Pacific, where he covered the invasions in the Marianas, at Leyte, Iwo Jima, and Okinawa. He was with the troops that occupied Japan and was present when the Japanese Premier Tojo attempted suicide. After the war he continued to photograph for the *Saturday Evening Post* and other magazines.

LARRY BURROWS

Born in London, England, in 1926, Larry Burrows began working at sixteen as an assistant in the London bureau of *Life* magazine, where he assisted such combat photographers as George Silk, Carl Mydans, Bob Capa, George Rodgers, Ralph Morse, and Frank Scherschel whenever they were in the London lab. He was rejected for military service during World War II because of bad eyesight. Burrows became a *Life* photographer in 1949 and was based in London. His first experience with war photography came in 1956 during the Anglo-French invasion of Egypt. His work in that conflict established him as a top war photographer, and he covered every war from then on for *Life*. He was named Magazine Photographer of the Year in 1966. On his way to photograph the South Vietnamese Army's invasion of Laos on February 10, 1971, he died when his helicopter was hit by antiaircraft fire and crashed. Burrows had spent fifteen of his forty-four years covering war.

JOHN BUSHEMI

John Bushemi was born in Gary, Indiana, and began his career as a photographer working for the *Gary Post-Tribune*. He was drafted in July 1941 and assigned to a field artillery unit at Fort Bragg. Bushemi was sent to the Pacific theater in October 1942, and photographed engagements at New Georgia, Tarawa, Kwajelein, Guadalcanal, the Fijis, and New Caledonia. In February 1944, he went in with the fourth wave of infantrymen during the invasion of Eniwetok Atoll in the Marshalls. After the beachhead was secured, he advanced to photograph the results of strafing by American planes. The area was still under sporadic mortar fire, and Bushemi was hit. He was rushed to a navy transport, but he died within three hours.

ROBERT CAPA

Robert Capa was born Andrei Friedmann in 1913 in Budapest. He began work as a photographic assistant in Berlin in 1931. He then worked as a freelance photoreporter, covering the Spanish Civil War from the Loyalist side. During 1941 and early 1942 Capa photographed the Battle of Britain. He also photographed the Atlantic convoys, and in 1943 he covered American troops in combat in North Africa. By January 1944, when Capa was covering the Fifth Army as it fought its way up the Italian peninsula, he was working exclusively for *Life*. He covered the Anzio invasion in February 1944, and in June he photographed the D-Day invasion of Normandy by riding in with the first wave of attack troops. Capa then photographed the battles of Normandy, the fall of Cherbourg, and the liberation of Paris. Returning to the combat zone in January 1945, Capa photographed the Battle of the Bulge, and in April he parachuted into Germany with the first wave of attackers east of the Rhine. He photographed the collapse and surrender of German forces, and in May 1945, at Leipzig, photographed an American machine gunner killed just minutes before the end of the war. After the war Capa helped found the Magnum photo agency. In 1954 he took his Leica to Vietnam to photograph the French army's fight against the Viet Mihn. Capa stepped on a land mine and, after eighteen years of photographing war, he was killed instantly. Capa published six books: *Death in the Making* (1937), *Battle of Waterloo Road* (1941), *Slightly out of Focus* (1947), *The Russian Journal* (with John Steinbeck) (1948), *Report on Israel* (with Irwin Shaw) (1950), and *Images of War* (1964).

AL CHANG

Born in 1922 on the island of Owahu in Hawaii, Chang learned photography in high school. At eighteen he enlisted in the army and served as a combat photographer in the South Pacific. He remained in the army after the war's end and was assigned to *Stars and Stripes*. The army sent him to cover the fighting in Korea, where he took a memorable picture showing a GI consoling another soldier whose buddy had just been killed. The picture was nominated for a Pulitzer Prize in 1950, and was selected by Edward Steichen for his "Family of Man" exhibition. He then photographed the Vietnam War until he retired from the army as a sergeant in 1964. Hired by the Saigon bureau of the Associated Press, he covered many of the bloodiest battles for the next three years, during which he was wounded three times. A memorable picture shows Chang clutching his Nikon even though he has sustained severe head wounds. He retired in 1968 and became a civilian photographer at Schofield Barracks in Hawaii. His honors include the Bronze Star, the White House Press Photographers Award, and the Wharang Distinguished Service Medal with Gold Star from the Korean government.

DICKEY CHAPELLE

Dickey Chapelle was born in 1919 in Milwaukee. Intent on becoming an airplane designer, she attended the Massachusetts Institute of Technology. She left school after only one year and went to New York City to pursue her new-found interest in photography. Hired by *Woman's Day* magazine, she covered World War II from the woman's angle. In the South Pacific she took a picture which brought the war home to thousands of civilians—a picture of a blood-covered soldier entitled "The Dying Marine." In 1952 she parachuted with the U.S. Special Forces in Korea, and in November 1956, while photographing people attempting to climb over the Berlin Wall, Chapelle was captured and imprisoned in Hungary for fifty days. Later, she made five separate trips to Vietnam, covering eleven major campaigns. In October, 1965, while photographing five Marines on patrol near DaNang, she was killed when a Marine a few steps in front of her tripped the wire of a hidden booby trap. At forty-six, she became the first American female combat photographer to be killed in action. Her book *What's a Woman Doing Here?* was published in 1961. That year she was awarded the George Polk Memorial Award, and after her death she was cited with a special mention award by the Overseas Press Club.

GEORGE S. COOK

George Smith Cook was born in Stratford, Connecticut in 1819. Brought up in Newark, New Jersey, he left at age fourteen for the South, eventually moving to New Orleans. Cook was a painter but began to make daguerreotypes before 1843. He travelled throughout the South as a portrait photographer and teacher from 1845 to 1849, when he opened a gallery in Charleston, S.C. In 1851, he moved to New York to manage Mathew Brady's gallery. In mid 50s he opened galleries in New York, Philadelphia, and Chicago. At the outbreak of the Civil War, Cook returned to Charleston, where he photographed Fort Sumter's ironclads in action, and other scenes in and around Charleston. For his many outstanding photos showing Confederate troops, Cook was considered "the photographer of the Confederacy" by his contemporaries. Much of his early work, taken with a large format view camera, was destroyed by fire in 1864. In 1874 he opened a short-lived studio in New York, then returned to Charleston. Cook died in 1902 in Bon Air, near Richmond, Virginia.

J.F. COONLEY

In 1856, while painting landscapes in his native Syracuse, New York, Coonley met George N. Barnard, "the leading photographer of that city." For the next few months he colored portraits in oils for Barnard, painted, and learned the essentials of the photographic business. After the financial panic of 1857 he set up shop as a photographer, and in 1861 the E. & T.H. Anthony Company sent Coonley to Mathew Brady's New York Gallery to copy Brady's collection of portraits of distinguished people. The Civil War broke out while Coonley was in Washington, and he spent a hectic time making portraits of soldiers and civilian officials along with Barnard. In 1864 he received a contract from the Quartermaster General to photograph the railroads in the Nashville, Tennessee area, under the threat of raids and ambushes from General Hood's cavalry. The following spring, after Savannah was captured and Charleston was evacuated, Coonley sailed to Fort Sumter and photographed the raising of the American flag. He returned to Washington, D.C. after the war's end, and photographed, with David Woodbury's assistance, the final parade and mustering out of the Grand Army of the Republic.

JEAN COTE

Cote was born in Lowell, Massachusetts in January 1926. In 1943 he joined the navy. Stationed in Brunswick, Maine, he volunteered to work in the base photo lab even though he had had no photographic training. Later, he was sent to the navy's Aerial Photography School in Norfolk, Virginia and then to the Pensacola, Florida photo school. While stationed in Monterey, California, he took evening classes with Ansel Adams and Win Bullock. He was then sent to the special navy photography program supervised by Professor Fred Demarest at Syracuse University. During the Korean War, Cote did photo interpretation work at the Pentagon. In late 1964, while stationed at Clark Air Force Base in Luzon in the Philippines, he was told by an admiral of an impending invasion in Vietnam. The admiral told the Chief Photographer's Mate, "You'd be able to get some great pictures if you were there." So Cote went. He and fellow navy photographer Bob Moser hitched a ride to Saigon, found the assault ships and were in on the first navy landing outside of Danang. During his tour in Vietnam he estimated he used his Leica to take between fifteen thousand and twenty thousand pictures—mainly of the seven major U.S. marine assaults he covered. In 1967 his pictures earned him a Presidential Citation. He retired in 1970 and lives in Hawaii.

MYRON H. DAVIS

Myron H. Davis worked for *Life* magazine covering wartime Washington, D.C. for nearly two years during the early part of the war. In 1943 he spent a year in the South Pacific theater where he photographed the U.S. navy's sweep through the Islands. He photographed the aftermath of the battles at New Guinea, New Britain, and Cape Gloucester.

MAX DESFOR

Born in Brooklyn, New York, Desfor studied photography at Brooklyn College. In 1933 he joined Associated Press as a messenger, and in 1938 he was assigned to the agency's Baltimore bureau. The following year he was promoted to the Washington bureau, where he took first prize in the 1941 White House News Photographers Association contest. In 1944, Desfor was sent to the South Pacific, where he covered the marines on Guam and Okinawa. He was on the battleship *Missouri* in Tokyo Bay to photograph the signing of the Japanese surrender. Over the next several years Desfor photographed armed conflict in India, Kashmir, Burma, Afghanistan, Indonesia, and Pakistan. Three weeks after the outbreak of the Korean War, Desfor took his 4×5 Speed Graphic to the front lines with the U.S. Twenty-fourth Infantry Division. His work there earned him the 1951 Pulitzer Prize. He retired from the AP's New York City bureau in 1978.

LT. ADRIAN DUFF

Lt. Adrian Duff's birthdate and birthplace are unknown. Duff became a top military photographer in World War I. Twenty of his photos were selected by the War Department as being among the 136 best pictures taken by military photographers during the war. Assigned to the Thirty-eighth Infantry, Third Division, he photographed the entry of American troops into Alsace on May 29, 1918. He photographed battles and the wounded near the bombed-out town of Vaux late in July of that year. Assigned to the St. Mihiel campaign in September, he photographed German prisoners at the front lines, where he remained for the rest of the war. One of Duff's most memorable photos was taken just one week before the Armistice was signed, and portrays an old French couple in the Ardennes greeting American soldiers.

DAVID DOUGLAS DUNCAN

David Douglas Duncan was born in Kansas City, Missouri in 1916, and studied marine zoology and deep-sea diving at the University of Miami. He became interested in photography, and experimented with taking undersea pictures. In 1936 he became a boxer and fought in more than forty bouts. In 1941 he enlisted in the Marine Corps, and photographed many major engagements in the South Pacific. On Bougainville he joined a band of Fijian guerrillas who harassed the Japanese troops behind the lines. He flew twenty-eight combat missions over Okinawa, three of these in a stifling, plexiglass belly tank which he attached under the wing of a P38. On one flight his pilot was killed by a bursting shell, but Duncan, although wounded by flak himself, was able to bail out of the plane. Duncan was the highest decorated marine photographer of World War II, winning two Distinguished Flying Crosses, three Air Medals, six battle stars, and a Purple Heart. He achieved the rank of First Lieutenant. He joined *Life* magazine and later was sent to Korea to cover the fighting there. His pictures of the siege of Khesanh during the Vietnam War were outstanding. Duncan has published numerous books, including *This is War!* and *I Protest!* He also devoted several years to photographing Picasso in his studio. Duncan now lives in the south of France, where he continues to write prolifically.

ELIOT ELISOFON

Eliot Elisofon covered many battles in North Africa from November 1942 to May 1943. He photographed at Casablanca, Maknassy, Sened, El Guettar, Gafsa, and Cape Bon. The airplane meant to return him to the United States crashed and burned on takeoff, but Elisofon escaped with only minor injuries. Elisofon took some of the strongest photographs of the early fighting in World War Two, but during the final years he worked primarily in North America and in Sweden.

HORST FAAS

Horst Faas was born in Berlin in April 1933. He began his photographic career in 1952 with Keystone Picture Agency in Berlin. Four years later he joined the Berlin Associated Press bureau as a photographer, and was transferred to the Bonn bureau. His first experience as a combat photographer was in the Congo in 1960. Later, he covered the outbreak of fighting in Algeria and then was transferred to Vietnam. He won a Pulitizer Prize for combat photos taken in Vietnam in 1965. He won the Robert Capa award of the Overseas Press Club that same year for "superlative photography requiring exceptional courage and enterprise." *The New York Times* and *Time* magazine were united in naming him the top photographer of the Vietnam War. Since then Horst Faas has worked on a freelance basis for some of the most respected magazines and newspapers in the United States.

FRANK FILAN

Filan was born in Brooklyn, New York, in 1905, and joined the Associated Press in 1923. In 1942, while he was covering an inspection tour of west coast army flying fields, his airplane collided with another near Victorville, California. He parachuted to safety and was the sole survivor, as both planes crashed and burned. Transferred to the South Pacific, he was with the first Marine Corps assault waves to land on Tarawa. During the battle he rescued numerous marines who had been hit by gunfire before reaching the beach. He was commended by Fleet Admiral Chester Nimitz for his "inspired devotion to duty," and his photo of the Battle of Tarawa won the Pulitzer Prize in 1944. In 1946, while covering the Chinese Communists, his jeep overturned, fracturing his arm. Filan returned to the United States, and was assigned to the Los Angeles bureau of AP, where he covered events in Hollywood until he became ill in 1951. Tragically, Filan died in Los Angeles on July 23, 1952, at the age of forty-seven.

ALEXANDER GARDNER

Alexander Gardner was born in 1821 in Paisley, Scotland. He studied physics, chemistry, and photography, and became a reporter and editor for the *Glasgow Sentinel*. Having moved to New York in 1856, he soon found employment in Mathew Brady's gallery. In early 1862 he joined the staff of General George B. McClellan of the Army of the Potomac, and, along with several other photographers, he recorded scenes and sites of McClellan's Penisular campaign. Gardner is given credit for three-fourths of the photographs of the Army of the Potomac. In September 1862, Gardner and James F. Gibson photographed the aftermath of the battle of Antietam. These photographs contained the first images of dead soldiers, and they caused a tremendous public response when displayed at Brady's studio in New York. In July 1863, Gardner opened his own studio and learned that General Lee was striking north into Pennsylavania and that a battle was likely to occur near Gettysburg. He arrived in time to make a series of photographs that show the destructiveness of war with unparalleled immediacy and force. In the late 1860s Gardner produced a variety of photographic albums from his own negatives or from the negatives of individuals that he sponsored. He died in 1882.

JAMES F. GIBSON

James F. Gibson was born in New York City early in the 1840s. He went to work at the Brady studio in New York, where he learned photography, and then transferred to the Washington studio under the direction of Alexander Gardner. He worked as a photographer out of Brady's Washington gallery in 1860–62. In March 1862 Gibson helped George N. Barnard photograph the site of the First Battle of Bull Run, which had occurred eight months earlier. In April the Union General George McClellan launched the Peninsular Campaign which led to the Battle of Fair Oaks in May, the retreat of Confederate forces, the Confederate counterattack under Robert E. Lee and the Seven Days Battles in June, the Battle of Gaines Mill, the attack on Savage's Station, and the battle at Malvern Hill in July. Gibson and John Wood followed closely in the train of the Union Army during these months, and produced the first photographs taken in the midst of an active field campaign. In September 1862, Gibson and Alexander Gardner reached the battlefield at Antietam and produced the first photographs of dead soldiers. In July 1863 Gibson was with Gardner and Timothy O'Sullivan at the battlefield at Gettysburg. During 1863 and 1864 Gibson photographed at Fredericksburg, Brandy Station, and elsewhere in Virginia.

RIDGEWAY GLOVER

Born in about 1848 in Philadelphia, Glover studied photography at a young age. In the summer of 1866 he headed west to take pictures which would "illustrate the life and character of the wild men of the prairie." He first worked for the *Philadelphia Photographer*, which ran a series of letters about his adventures. Early in July 1866, he joined an army train which, escorted by five officers and a detachment of the Eighteenth Infantry, set out from Laramie for Fort Kearney. The group was attacked by Indians and one officer was killed. Glover took a number of photos while at Fort Kearney and on October 27, 1866, *Leslie's Illustrated Weekly* said that Ridgeway was a special correspondent representing the paper in the West. While photographing an area near the fort on September 14, 1866, Glover was killed by Sioux warriors.

STAN GROSSFELD

Grossfeld was born in 1951 in Bronx, New York. He began his photographic career in 1973 on the *Newark Star-Ledger*. Two years later, he joined the *Boston Globe* and worked his way up to Associate Editor. He won two consecutive Pulitzer Prizes in 1984 and 1985 for his photography in Ethiopia and in Lebanon. He also won two consecutive Overseas Press Club Awards. His pictures taken during the Persian Gulf War, showing the remains of an Iraqi soldier in a bombed-out van has been called the most graphic of any published in the U.S.A.

A graduate of Boston University's College of Communication, Grossfeld is the author of *Nantucket: The Other Season*, *The Eyes of the Globe*, and *Two on the River*.

JAMES HENRY HARE

James Henry Hare was born in 1856 in London. He attended St. John's College in London for about a year in 1871 and then became an apprentice to his father, who made photographic apparatus. Hare went to New York in 1889 as a technical advisor to E. & H.T. Anthony & Co. In February 1898 he joined *Collier's Weekly* to cover the Spanish-American War in Cuba. He landed secretly in Cuba and photographed the soldiers of Maximo Gomez's guerilla force during the first months of the war, then photographed American military preparations and, in July 1898, he photographed aspects of the battle of San Juan while under fire with the correspondent Stephen Crane. From 1898 until 1914 Hare worked for *Collier's Weekly*, photographing the Russo-Japanese War in 1904, such news events in the United States as the experiments with powered flight by the Wright brothers and others in the teens, the first Balkan War in 1912, and the Mexican Revolution in 1911 and again in 1914. In 1918 the Italians invited Hare to cover the war in Italy. He responded immediately and photographed the Italians under attack that summer and the counteroffensive Italy launched in October 1918, which eventually knocked the Austrians out of the war. With Cecil Carnes, he wrote *Jimmy Hare News Photographer: Half a Century with a Camera*. He died in June, 1946 at the age of 89.

NORMAN T. HATCH

Born in Boston on March 2, 1921, he enlisted in the Marine Corps immediately after graduating from Gloucester High School. He was sent to the March of Time School of Pictorial Journalism in New York City. Hatch went with the Second Marine Division to New Zealand and landed with one of the first waves on Tarawa. He was promoted to sergeant and was sent back to the United States to show his pictures from Tarawa and participate in the Fourth War Loan Drive. Hatch was promoted to Warrant Officer and served as photo officer during the invasion of Iwo Jima. Later he was in on the invasions of Saipan and Okinawa, and received the Presidential Unit Citation and the Bronze Star. After the war he became head of the Audio-Visual Division, Office of Public Affairs, Office of the Secretary of Defense. He retired in January of 1979.

JOHN C. HEMMENT

John C. Hemment was born in New York City in about 1873. He studied photography and, while in his early twenties, established a photo studio in Brooklyn. On the side, he did a considerable amount of photo work for *Leslie's Illustrated Weekly*. The U.S. government sent Hemment to Cuba prior to the Spanish-American War to take pictures of the battleship *Maine* stranded in Havana Harbor after the explosion aboard.

Instead of returning immediately to the United States, he lingered and photographed the Spanish fortifications. Caught in the act, he was arrested as a spy. He wrote that he was able to escape prosecution by bribing a guard. In Santiago, he took some early aerial reconnaissance photographs—pictures from a balloon of Spanish trenches and fortifications. His pictures included the wreckage of the *Maine*, fortifications at Havana Harbor, the Rough Riders, Morro Castle, aerial photos of Spanish trenches, and American warships. Hemment returned to New York on September 3 on the same ship with Teddy Roosevelt's Rough Riders. In 1900 the *New York Journal* called him "the photographer who gave the American people the only pictorial record of the triumph of American arms over the Spanish in Cuba." He died in 1927.

HENRI HUET

Born in 1927 in Delat, South Vietnam, Huet grew up in France where he studied art and photography. He took specialized courses at the French Army School of Photography and covered action in North Vietnam for three years. For the next nine years he was a photographer for the United States Information Service. He then joined the Saigon Bureau of The Associated Press. At great personal risk, Huet took pictures of the battle of An Thi between Viet Cong and First Air Cavalry troops in January 1966. These pictures were among those which won him the Overseas Press Club's 1967 Robert Capa Gold Medal Award for "superlative still photography requiring exceptional courage and enterprise." Huet is credited with helping carry a wounded American one hundred yards [90m] through a rice paddy while under fire. Lt. Col. Robert McDade, a battalion commander of the First Air Cavalry, called Huet "one of the bravest men I've ever seen." Huet was killed in action on February 10, 1971, when his helicopter crashed in Laos.

WILLIAM H. ILLINGWORTH

William Illingworth was born in England in 1844. His family emigrated to the United States when he was a child, and he grew up in Philadelphia and in St. Paul, Minnesota, where his father had a small jewelry business. At twenty, Illingworth moved to Chicago, where he learned photography, possibly from John Carbutt. In 1866 he accompanied Captain Fisk's expedition into the Montana territory where he took at least thirty stereoscopic views that were distributed by Carbutt. In 1874 he ventured into the Black Hills with General George Custer's expedition, where he made almost one hundred images of the scenery and of the expedition's activities. Custer's first expedition did not run up against hostile action however, and Illingworth did not photograph any Indians. In 1893, after several years of depression, Illingworth shot and killed himself.

WILLIAM HENRY JACKSON

Born in Omaha, Nebraska in 1843, Jackson served in the Civll War, but not as a photographer. He became

a professional photographer in Omaha in 1868 at age 25. The following year he met Dr. F.V. Hayden who made him the official photographer for his ten-year survey of the West. While travelling with Hayden, Jackson photographed many Indians, including Washakie, the famous Shoshone chief. His photographs of Yellowstone were instrumental in influencing Congress to declare it a National Park. Historian Robert Taft calls Jackson the "most outstanding of all frontier photographers."

FRANCES BENJAMIN JOHNSTON

Frances Benjamin Johnston was born on Janaury 15, 1864 in Grafton, West Virginia. After studying art in Paris, she became a newspaper columnist in Washington, D. C. She began photographing professionally in 1888 and quickly developed a reputation as a news and feature photographer. She became the first American woman war photographer when she covered the Spanish-American War. Her most notable pictures were made aboard the USS *Olympia*, Admiral Dewey's flagship, on the occasion of his victorious return to the United States in 1899. In 1900 a portfolio of her photographs was exhibited at the International Congress of Photography in Paris, to which Miss Johnston was the only woman delegate. She died in 1952, and an extensive collection of her photographs, including her Spanish-American War pictures, is in the Library of Congress.

SERGEANT JERRY JOSWICK

Jerry Joswick was born in 1920 in Chicago and became a studio photographer in Chicago. He enlisted in the army a few days after the attack on Pearl Harbor, received training at Bolling Field near Washington, and was sent to Cairo in January 1943. Joswick was the only photographer to return from the air raid on the Ploesti oil fields. His commander, Lt. Col. John D. Craig, says of him, "He was ready to fly in any kind of aricraft and liked to ride that 'Purple Heart' location: the high, outside left wing slip from which he could best photograph fighter attacks." He covered the invasion of France on Omaha Beach on June 6, 1944. A few days later he was captured, but was released because prisoners would slow the retreat. He became the most heavily decorated army photographer in World War II, winning two Distinguished Flying Crosses, the Air Medal, and the Bronze Star while a member of the Ninth Combat Camera Unit in Africa, Italy, and France. After the war, he filmed the atomic bomb blast at Bikini and finally settled in Barrington, Illinois, where he became a television producer.

DAVID HUME KENNERLY

The winner of the 1972 Pulitzer Prize for his Vietnam coverage was born on March 9, 1947 in Rosebud, Oregon. He enrolled in Postland State College but quit after a year to become a staff photographer on the Oregon *Journal*. After a year he went to the Portland *Oregonian* and, after another year, to the United Press

International bureau in Los Angeles. In March 1971 he was sent to UPI's Saigon bureau. He became the last photographer hired before *Life* magazine folded, and he stayed on with *Time* magazine—photographing twenty-five covers. After being President Gerald Ford's White House photographer, he returned to *Time* and covered such trouble spots as Mozambique, Northern Ireland, El Salvador, Beirut, and the Southern Sahara. Besides the Pulitzer, his other honors include awards from the White House Press Photographers, the Overseas Press Club, the National Press Photographers, and the World Press Association. He was executive producer and co-writer of the NBC movie based on his autobiographical book, *Shooter*, which detailed his Vietnam experiences. Another book, *Photo Op*, was published in 1995. Kennerly lives in Santa Monica, California with his wife, screenwriter Rebecca Soladay, and two sons.

FRANK KERR

The man who was to become the top Marine Corps photographer in Korea was born in Seattle, Washington on March 12, 1930. He enlisted in the Marine Corps in 1948 and he was one of the first Marine photographers to be sent to cover the Korean War. One of his picture-stories, "The Ordeal of Marine Squad II," was sent back to Marine Headquarters in Washington, where it was noticed by a *Saturday Evening Post* editor and subsequently published. A group of Marine Corps photo officers in the Pentagon selected Kerr's pictures as the best taken in Korea. Even though he was a Marine, he was awarded a formal commendation from the U.S. Army. After the war he joined the photo staff of the *Boston Herald-American*, and later became a photographer for United Press International. In 1954 he became a reporter for United Press International. He went on to write television documentaries, including the award-winning "Friendship Seven," the story of John Glenn's space adventure. Kerr is now a partner in the Boston public relations firm of Schofield & Co. He is the founding president of The Chosin Few, an organization made up of veterans of the Chosin campaign in Korea.

LOU LOWERY

Born in Pittsburgh, Pennsylvania on July 24, 1916, Lowery worked as a photographer on the *Pittsburgh Post Gazette*, and began his own commercial photography firm. He joined the marines in 1943, and was taken out of boot camp to be a correspondent for *Leatherneck* magazine in the South Pacific. He went in on six major landings—more than any other photographer. On Iwo Jima, he photographed the raising of the first flag. He received two Purple Hearts for his wounds. After the war he stayed with *Leatherneck* as director of photography. He retired in 1982 as a captain in the Marine Corps Reserves.

A.J. LYTLE

Lytle was born in the early 1840s in Baton Rouge, Louisiana. Shortly before the beginning of the Civil War,

he established a photographic studio on Main Street in Baton Rouge. During the war he was in the employment of the Confederate Secret Service and became known as history's first spy photographer. A Lytle photo of the First Indiana Heavy Artillery Brigade published in the *Photographic History of the Civil War* was captioned, "one of the many [photos] made by A.D. [sic.] Lytle in Baton Rouge during its occupancy by the Federals. This Confederate photographer risked his life to obtain negatives of Federal batteries, cavalry regiments and camps, lookout towers, and the vessels of Farragut and Porter, in fact of everything that might be of the slightest use in informing the Confederate Secret Service of the strength of the Federal occupation of Baton Rouge." Lytle's son told historian Henry Wysham Lanier in 1911 that his father used a signal with a flag and lantern from the observation tower on Scott's Bluff, from which point the coded message would be relayed to the Confederates near New Orleans. But Northern sharpshooters soon spotted him so he had to discontinue his work.

RALPH MORSE

Ralph Morse was born in Bronx, New York. After graduating from school he took a brief course in photography at the City College of New York, and worked as an errand boy at the Paul Parker Studio. Morse freelanced and had his first *Life* assignment in 1938; he joined the *Life* staff in 1942. He spent fourteen months in the South Pacific for Life, and sailed to Hawaii two months after the attack in December, 1941. He photographed a major feature story "Hawaii at War" in early 1942. Joining the naval fleet, Morse covered the sea battle at Midway from aboard a cruiser. He also photographed the marine invasion of Guadalcanal. During the first battle of Savo Island, the heavy cruiser that Morse was on, the USS *Vincennes*, was sunk. Morse floated in the ocean for six and a half hours before being rescued, and he lost all of his cameras and equipment. After being rescued, Morse spent nine days on a hospital ship, where he produced one of his better photo essays. In November and December 1942 he returned to photograph the fighting on Guadalcanal. He was transferred to the European Theatre where he photographed the Allied armada during the Normandy invasion, then followed the fighting in France and Germany until the end of the war.

HUYNH THANH MY

Huynh Thanh My was born in 1936 in the Mekong Delta of Vietnam, and photographed French troops fighting in what was then French Indochina. When American troops were sent to Vietnam, My got a job photographing the war for an American television network. In 1964 his work was so appreciated by Horst Faas that Faas lured him to the Associated Press Saigon Bureau. My was wounded in action May 27, 1965. Although bleeding profusely, he kept taking pictures until he could no longer work the shutter. He then handed his camera to a soldier to record more pictures of the battle, including a few of

My himself. Later, he was beaten both by rioters and police in a Saigon demonstration. He covered battles in the Mekong Delta and the jungles of Zone D and Phuoc Tuy. While photographing American troops on October 13, 1965, My was killed in action. My was given a posthumous award for valor in the Thirty-second Annual Headliners Club competition.

CARL MYDANS

Carl Mydans was born in Boston in 1907 and graduated from Boston University's College of Communication. He worked as a reporter on the *Boston Herald* and the *Boston Globe*. He was hired by Roy Stryker as a Farm Security Administration photographer, then by Henry Luce in 1936 as one of the first photographers on *Life* magazine. In 1941 he covered Burma, Malaya and the Philippines. On January 2, 1942 he was taken prisoner along with his wife by the Japanese in Manila. His captors offered them freedom if Mydans would become a photographer for the Japanese. He refused. He and his wife were exchanged in October 1943, after being held prisoners almost two years. Mydans covered the North African campaign, then, with Slim Aarons of *Yank* magazine and fellow *Life* photographer George Silk, photographed the Italian campaigns near Rome, Florence, and Cassino. He later covered the invasion of Southern France. Returning to the Pacific theater, he landed with marines on Luzon and photographed the fall of the very prison camp in which he had been a prisoner. He covered the surrender of Japan aboard the battleship *Missouri* in Tokyo Bay. Together with Robert Capa he covered French forces fighting in Vietnam in 1948. Two years later he covered the Korean War. He wrote *More than Meets the Eye* in 1959 and *The Violent Press* in 1968. His Korean War pictures won the U.S. Camera Gold Achievement Award in 1950. In 1960 he received an honorary doctorate in humanities from Boston University. He's now retired and living in a New York suburb.

FRANK NOEL

Born in Delhart, Texas on February 12, 1905, Frank Noel began his photographic career on the staff of the *Chicago Daily News* at age twenty. In 1928 he enlisted in the Army Air Corps and served as an instructor in aerial photography. When his term of service was over, he joined the staff of the *Washington Post*. On January ll, 1937, he joined the Associated Press and after working in Atlanta and Miami, was transferred to New York prior to foreign assignment in September 1941. Near the end of the of that year, his ship was torpedoed off Sumatra by the Japanese and his lifeboat drifted for about six weeks in the Indian Ocean. Prior to reaching safety on January 20, 1942, he made a Pulitzer Prize-winning photograph of an East Indian sailor on another lifeboat pleading for a drink of water. Noel covered the Palestine conflict in May 1948 and was transferred to Berlin in 1949. He arrived in Korea a month after hostilities began, saw action in the front lines, and was captured by the Communists near the Changjin Reservoir on November 29, 1950. Almost three years later, on August 9, 1953, he was released and returned to the wire photo desk in New York. While in the prisoner-of-war camp, he had the rare opportunity to take a number of photographs of fellow prisoners. Noel retired from the AP in May 1966. He died in 1981 at age seventy-six.

JOHN OLSON

Born on March 7, 1947 in Evanston, Illinois, John Olson was employed as a photographer for the *Minnetonka Herald* at fourteen, after his family had moved to Wayzata, Minnesota. Later, he worked for UPI and the *Minneapolis Tribune*. Drafted in 1966, he volunteered for duty in Vietnam. He was on the staff of *Stars and Stripes*, and photographed some of the bitterest battles of the war. He spent two years photographing the war and was wounded twice. His pictures of the fight for Hue during the Tet offensive were published in *Life* magazine on March 8, 1968. After his discharge, he became the youngest photographer to join the staff of *Life* magazine. His series entitled "The Battle that Regained and Ruined Hue" won the Robert Capa award for "superlative still photography requiring exceptional courage and enterprise abroad."

TIMOTHY O'SULLIVAN

Timothy O'Sullivan was born in New York City around 1840. By his mid-teens O'Sullivan was working in Mathew Brady's New York studio; he subsequently joined Brady's staff in the Washington, D.C. gallery. From December 1861 to May 1862 O'Sullivan held the rank of First Lieutenant and photographed near Beaufort and Port Royal, the islands along the Carolina coast and around Fort Walker and Fort Pulaski, Georgia. In May he was honorably discharged and rejoined Brady's staff. In July 1862 O'Sullivan followed General John Pope's invasion into Virginia and photographed military bridges, railroad depots, and scenes around Manassas and Culpeper. O'Sullivan photographed troops deployed for the battle at Fredericksburg in May 1863. In July, he was with Alexander Gardner and James Gibson at Gettysburg, photographing the site before the dead could be buried. "The Harvest of Death," which he took at Gettysburg, is one of the most famous of Civil War pictures. In 1864 he covered the opening of Grant's Spring campaign against Lee in Northern Virginia, then the siege of Petersburg, operations against Fort Fischer, North Carolina, in December 1864, and the end of the conflict at Appomattox Court House in April 1865. That year, Gardner published his two volume set of original photographs, the *Photographic Sketchbook of the War*, with forty-four of the one hundred photographs credited to O'Sullivan. He died on January 14, 1882 at the age of forty-two.

TIM PAGE

Tim Page was born in London in 1948. He left at the age of seventeen to "see the world," In 1965 he found himself in the middle of a small, unknown civil war in Laos. He took some pictures and sold them to United Press International. Thus he began his career as a combat photographer. During the next five years he worked on assignments in a number of troubled countries, covering the Six-day War in the Near East in 1967 for Time-Life and working in Vietnam on a freelance basis for all of the major wire services and most of the major magazines. Page was in Vietnam from the earliest period of the American involvement in that conflict, and his actions were considered by those who knew him as daring and extreme. Page was featured in several articles on the war by his friend and fellow correspondent Michael Herr, the author of *Dispatches*, and his character has been broadly assumed to be the basis for the role of the photojournalist in the movie "Apocalypse Now. " Continually seeking combat, Page was severely wounded a number of times. He has been the subject of a BBC doumentary film "Mentioned In Dispaches." His book *Tim Page's Nam* was published in 1983. He has returned to London where he is currently freelancing.

JAMES PICKERELL

Born in 1937 in Wilmington, Ohio, James Pickerell joined the U.S. navy in l955 and was trained to be a photographer. After his discharge, he graduated from UCLA and went to Tokyo as a freelance photographer. When the Vietnam War broke out, Pickerell was offered transportation to Saigon and a job by United Press International. On his very first day in Saigon, he came across a group of Buddhists who were demonstrating against the government of President Ngo Dinh Diem, and he shot twenty-five rolls of film. One of those pictures made the cover of *Life* magazine. A friend commented, "What a way to start a career—first story shot makes *Life*." As the war progressed and shifted to the swamps and mountain jungles, Pickerell followed the troops, and became the first American correspondent to be wounded in action in Vietnam. In September 1964, he went back to the front lines again, and one of his pictures made a *Newsweek* cover. In the year that followed, he got five more covers. On one memorable occasion, he was taking pictures of a suspect being interrogated, when he heard a Vietnamese officer say to an American officer, "I think I'll shoot this man." Pickerell spun around and snapped a picture just as the Vietnamese raised his carbine and shot the prisoner through the head. He now has a studio in Washington.

CO RENTMEESTER

Co Rentmeester was born in Amsterdam, Holland in 1936. He emigrated to the United States in order to study photography at the Los Angeles Art Center School, where he received his degree in 1965. Rentmeester began his professional career freelancing for *Life* magazine, and in 1966 joined the staff to cover the war in Vietnam. His powerful series of photographs of a battle-weary tank crew won the 1967 World Press Photo Grand Prize. In late 1967 he was wounded by a Vietcong sniper during a battle near Saigon. He was reassigned to the United States in 1969. For his non-combat work he continued to win awards throughout his career: in 1972 he won the "Magazine Photographer of the Year" award and the best sports picture award of the World Press Photo Foundation. In 1980 he won awards from the University of Missouri School of Journalism and from the World Press Photo Foundation. He shot a major feature on supersonic jet fighters which appeared in *American Photographer* magazine in 1984. He has written a book, *Three Faces of Indonesia*. He is now a New York freelancer in the area of fashion photography.

JOHN ROBATON

Born in Hershey, Pennsylvania. on June 26, 1940, Robaton earned a Master's degree in photojournalism at Boston University in 1965. He joined United Press International in San Francisco before freelancing in Europe and Japan. In 1970 he was sent to cover the Vietnam War by *Newsweek* magazine. He covered action all over Southeast Asia but received the most acclaim for his pictures during the period of the Cambodian invasion. He returned to New York to freelance and is now a professor of photojournalism at Boston University.

THOMAS C. ROCHE

Thomas C. Roche was one of the most active and prolific photographers of the Civil War, and he was described in the *Photographic History of the Civil War* as "an indefatigable worker in the army's train." He was affiliated briefly with Mathew Brady, and later with Alexander Gardner. He worked for the Quartermaster Corps and it is possible that he photographed under the direction of Captain Andrew Russell later in the war. Toward the end of the war he photographed the Battle of Dutch Gap Canal while under cannon fire. Roche's most powerful and disturbing series of photographs was of the corpses of Confederate soldiers lying in the trenches before Petersburg in April 1865.

JOE ROSENTHAL

The man who took the most acclaimed war photograph of all time was born in Washington, D.C. in 1912. His family moved to California, where he took up photography as a hobby. When World War II broke out he joined the U.S. Maritime Service and was soon promoted to the rank of Chief Photographer's Mate. Within two years, however, he was discharged because of poor eyesight—an ailment that would continue to plague him throughout his life. Nonetheless, in February 1944 he joined the Associated Press in San Francisco, and the following month was sent to cover the war in the Pacific. There he photographed action in the Solomons, Hollandia, Guadalcanal, Guam, Marianas, the Phillpines, and Iwo Jima. Rosenthal landed on Iwo Jima on February 19, 1945. During the eleven days Rosenthal spent there he made sixty-five photographs with his 4 × 5 Speed Graphic. On February 23, he photographed Marines erecting a flag on Mt. Suribachi. The flag-raising picture was placed on more front pages than any other news picture, and stirred up a response unprecedented in the history of American press photography. The photo was used as a model for a national monument erected near Washington, D.C. Ironically, when informed he had won the 1945 Pulitzer Prize, Rosenthal thought it might have been for another picture because, thanks to his poor eyesight, he wasn't sure the flag raising picture had been in focus. After the war he joined the staff of the *San Francisco Chronicle*, where he worked until his retirement in 1982.

ANDREW JOSEPH RUSSELL

Andrew Russell was born in Nunda, New York. Early on, he showed artistic talent, and he taught penmanship in the Nunda public school before he left to set up a studio in New York. He learned photography and used it to help with his paintings. In the 1860s Russell displayed the paintings including landscapes and genre scenes of "dying civil war soldiers" in various exhibitions. In 1862 Russell enlisted in the Union army, joining the 141st New York volunteers. He was assigned to the U.S. Military Railroad Construction Corps under General Haupt. Russell led a team that documented the bridges, railroad construction, camps, and other projects of that corps. Russell also documented such military activities, battlefields, and combat aftermath scenes as were available to him during the war. He made some particularly powerful images at Marye's Heights during the battle of Fredericksburg. He also photographed at Petersburg, Alexandria, and at the fall of Richmond. After the war, Russell became the official photographer for the Union Pacific Railroad, and he led a crew that photographed construction from 1867 to 1869. At the ceremony at Promontory Point, Utah, that joined the rails of the Union Pacific and the Central Pacific, Russell took the famous photograph of the golden spike being driven. In 1870, he returned to New York and established a studio. He retired to Brooklyn in 1891, and died there in 1902.

TOSHIO SAKAI

Sakai was born in Tokyo in 1933, and graduated from Tokyo's Meiji University with a major in economics. He joined United Press International in 1965 as a staff photographer, and was assigned to cover the Vietnam War in 1967. In 1973 he was made picture editor of the Saigon Bureau handling all of Southeast Asia. In 1975, he was transferred to the Seoul Bureau, and in 1977 he left UPI to become a freelancer. In 1967, his picture of American GIs trying to sleep despite a rainstorm, entitled "Dreams of a Better World" won the Pulitzer Prize for feature photography. He now lives in Tokyo where he is a freelance photographer.

KYOICHI SAWADA

Born in Aomori, Japan in 1936, Kyoichi Sawada bought his first box camera for $1.65 when he was thir-

teen, with money he earned selling newspapaers. At twenty, he had his own photography concession at a U.S. airbase in Japan where he learned to speak English. In 1960, he joined the Tokyo staff of United Press International and went to Vietnam at his own request early in 1965. On one occasion, he preceded attacking U.S. troops so he could get full front shots of them charging into combat. He was later reprimanded for entering a mine field to photograph U.S. infantrymen. His Vietnam coverage won five major awards: the main prize at the tenth Annual World Press Photo Exhibition at The Hague, Netherlands in both 1965 and 1966; the 1966 and 1967 Overseas Press Club award for the year's best wire service photographic reporting from abroad; and the 1966 Pulitzer Prize for news photography for his picture, "Flee to Safety." On October 18, 1970, he was killed in a Communist ambush near Phnom Penh.

SAMUEL SCHULMAN

Born in 1903 in Brooklyn, New York, Schulman attended Hebrew Technical Institute in Brooklyn. In 1920, he got a job as a copy boy on the *New York American*. He taught himself photography and, in 1922, became a staff photographer on the paper. He covered the White House and photographed presidents Coolidge, Hoover, and Roosevelt. He joined the International News Service and, at the outbreak of World War II, went to cover the action in North Africa and Europe. He once wrote, "If, in peace, a picture is worth 10,000 words, a war picture must be worth 100,000, for it conveys at a single glance an emotion which takes so many, many words to convey—the emotion of horror." Schulman was the subject of the book *Where's Sammy?*, by Bob Considine. After the war, he became a freelance photographer with a studio in New York City.

GEORGE SILK

Silk was born in Sydney, Australia in 1917. At the age of fourteen, he dropped out of high school to take a job developing and printing pictures in a photo shop. In 1940, after the British Empire went to war, Silk was about to be drafted. "Since I preferred going to war as a photographer rather than an an infantryman, I got a job with the Australian Ministry of War," he said. "I was sent with the Australian Army to the Middle East: Greece and Crete. Things got so bad there, I was sent to New Guinea and went with a regiment on that terribly long trek to Port Moresby. Although we were able to push the Japanese back, this was the toughest campaign of the whole war," he said. "At the end of this campaign, only ten percent of the men were still on their feet," he recalled. But his pictures of the Burma campaign attracted the attention of *Life*. He joined the magazine in 1943 and was sent to the Italian front. He remained in Europe eighteen months photographing the war. In February, 1945, while photographing the American Ninth Army's drive for the Rhine, he was wounded in the leg by fragments of an exploding grenade thrown by a captured German tank crew member. After recovering from his

wounds he was sent to the Pacific shortly before V-J Day. There he flew several aerial missions from the aircraft carrier, *Ticonderoga*.

W. EUGENE SMITH

Smith was born in Wichita, Kansas in 1918 and studied photography while in high school. He attended Notre Dame on a photography scholarship set up especially for him. After a year of college he joined *Newsweek* magazine in 1936, but was fired for using a "miniature" camera ($2\frac{1}{4} \times 2\frac{1}{4}$) after being given orders not to. Then, in rapid succession, he worked for *Life*, *Collier's*, *American*, and the *New York Times*. When the United States entered World War II in 1941, he became a combat photographer, first for Ziff-Davis and later for *Life*. After covering the war in the Atlantic in 1942, he was transferred to the South Pacific, where he was involved in twenty-six carrier combat missions and thirteen invasions. He went in on Okinawa, and then hitched rides twelve hundred miles to Guam to be certain his pictures would be flown to Life as soon as possible. He returned to Okinawa where, while photographing an essay entitled "A Day in the Life of a Front Life Soldier," he was seriously wounded by Japanese shell fragments. In 1955, he became a Magnum photographer and did exceptional photo essays on Pittsburgh and Hiroshima victims of mercury poisoning. He died in 1973.

WILLIAM STINSON SOULE

Wiliam Soule was born in Maine in 1836. He was the younger brother of John P. Soule, a well-known Boston photographer. During the Civil War, he joined a Massachusetts regiment and was badly wounded at Antietam. He worked for the balance of the war as a clerk in Washington, D.C. He then worked in a photographic gallery in Chambersburgh, Pennsylvania until the gallery burned in 1866. Soule then went west to improve his health, which was still affected by his wound. He worked as a clerk in the post store at Fort Dodge, Kansas and occasionally took photographs. In 1868 Soule moved to the new military base, Camp Supply, and then on to the newly constructed Fort Sill in the Indian Territory. He ran a photographic gallery there until about 1875. Fort Sill was the Indian Agency and Military Control Headquarters for most of the Southern Plains Tribes, and Soule built up a major body of portraits of a wide variety of tribes. In 1875, Soule left the Indian Territory and returned to Boston, where he continued to maintain a professional studio until 1902. He died in 1908.

PETER STACKPOLE

Born in Oakland, California in 1913, Peter Stackpole began experimenting with an early model Leica while in technical high school. In 1935, just four years out of high school, he attracted attention with his photographs of the building of the Golden Gate and Oakland-San Francisco Bay suspension bridges. A year later, he was hired by *Life* magazine and his name appears as a staff photographer on the masthead of the first issue. During World War II he photographed the marines in the South Pacific. He won the 1953 George Polk Memorial Award for News Photography.

EDWARD STEICHEN

Ten years before Edward Steichen enlisted in the army during World War I at age thirty-five, London reviewer A.C.R. Carter wrote, "Is photography an art? Let the answer be, 'Yes, if it's Steichen.'" He had been one of America's leading commercial photographers before the war which would bring him fame as an outstanding combat photographer. Steichen's work at the front won him several promotions, and by the end of the war he was a full colonel. Although sixty-one years old when World War II broke out, Steichen was eager to participate in creating a photographic record of the war. His felt that "...if we could really photograph war as it was...in all its monstrous actuality, that could be a great deterrent for war." His age kept him out of the army, but he convinced the navy to let him enlist. Pictures taken by Steichen's unit were among the most outstanding of the war. After the war, while a photographic curator at the Museum of Modern Art in New York, he mounted the greatest collection of photography ever assembled, and called it "The Family of Man." He died in 1973.

DONALD C. THOMPSON

Donald C. Thompson was born in 1889 and grew up in Kansas. By 1914 he was working on a newspaper in Canada. When Germany declared war on Russia and then invaded Luxembourg in August of that year, Thompson "sold everything I had—pawned my watch and bought a complete photographic outfit and my steamship ticket" and sailed to London. He then left for Paris and from there traveled to the French front on his own authority. His first photographs were of British troops at the Battle of Mons. Thompson then went to Belgium, where he followed the Belgians through thirty-two battles until the fall of Antwerp. In February 1915 Thompson and Robert McCormick of the *Chicago Tribune* were invited to visit the different fronts in Russia. Thompson left for Russia, then Bulgaria, Serbia and Turkey. Returning through Italy, he was back on the French front in July 1916, when he was wounded by a shell fragment. Thompson was in Russia at the outbreak of the October Revolution, and for the next seven months photographed the course of the Revolution and the rise of the Communist Party to power.

EDWARD R. TRABOLD

A World War I Signal Corps photographer, Edward R. Trabold was stationed with the Second Field Signal Corps Battalion. Assigned to the First Division in France, he covered several major battles, including the attack on Cantigny. One of the numerous pictures taken by Trabold during this encounter is included in the War Department's list of the most outstanding photographs of World War I.

SLAVA VEDER

Born August 30, 1926 in Berkeley, California, Veder studied at Diablo Valley College and at Sacramento State College. In 1961 he was hired as an Associated Press photographer in Sacramento. Later he covered stories in Southeast Asia and Vietnam. His pictures of the first American coming home from Vietnam to Travis Air Force Base in California won first place in the University of Missouri National Press Photographers contest and a Pulitzer Prize for feature photography in 1974. He is married and lives in Martinez, California.

HANK WALKER

Born in Canada in 1922, Walker moved to Los Angeles as a youth and studied photography. He worked on the *San Francisco Examiner* and a few magazines before World War II. From 1943 to 1945 he saw action as a marine combat photographer with the Fifth Amphibious Corps on Saipan and Tinian. Walker became a *Life* "stringer" after the war and covered such assignments as the Berlin Air Lift. He was put on the *Life* staff full-time in May 1950, and three months later was sent to cover the Korean War. He is best known for his combat pictures of the landing at Inchon and the capture of the Kimpo airfield. He later worked for the *Saturday Evening Post* before going to Florida to work for a radio station.

CAPTAIN HERMAN V. WALL

Herman V. Wall was born in 1905 in Milwaukee. In 1926, his family moved to Los Angeles, where he attended the Art Center School and became an instructor in photography. At the beginning of World War II he was given a commission to be a photography officer. In England in early June of 1944, he heard of the impending invasion of Normandy and volunteered to go in with one of the first waves. His request was granted and he led his command, the 165th Signal Photo Company, into battle on D-Day minus six. He was one of the first photographers to reach the beach and take pictures of the American troops coming ashore. His company sustained heavy casualties—forty-eight percent of all Signal Corps personnel participating in the invasion were either killed, wounded or captured. Joined by *Yank* magazine photographer Sergeant Pete Parris, Captain Wall climbed to higher ground to be able to get better pictures just as a shell fell in their midst. Parris was killed instantly and Wall was severly wounded.

Later that day Wall was taken out to a British ship where his left leg, already badly mutilated, was amputated. He somehow had been able to hang on to his Leica, which contained priceless photos of the invasion. Eventually, the Army Pictorial Service in London received, processed, and distributed his pictures—the first back from the invasion. He was awarded the Legion of Merit and the Purple Heart. He retired as a major in 1945 and returned to work as an advertising photographer in Los Angeles. For twenty-five years he has worked with new and prospective amputees at the UCLA Medical Center, giving them the benefit of his experience as an amputee.

JOHN T. WHEELER

Born in El Paso, Texas in 1930, Wheeler attended the University of Missouri School of Journalism and, after working for several newspapers, joined the Associated Press in San Francisco in 1959. In 1962 he volunteered for duty in Southeast Asia and was sent to Kuala Lumpur before being assigned to Saigon in early 1965. After helping wounded soldiers out of heavy Vietcong fire on April 21, 1965, he was publicly cited for bravery by the United States government. Earlier that year, while he was covering an operation with the American Twenty-fifth Division near CuChi on February 14, an American soldier threw a grenade which hit a tree and bounced back toward Wheeler before exploding and wounding him slightly. However, Wheeler was back in action the next day.

SCOTT WIGLE

Born in 1907 in Detroit, Michigan, Wigle became a reporter for the *Detroit Times* in 1936. He joined the coast guard in 1943 and was trained to be a photographer. During the war he documented the coast guard operations, but saw action in only one major battle—Normandy. One of his pictures became the first invasion picture to be radioed back to the United States and shows a long line of troop-filled vessels with barrage balloons trailing as the vessels anchored off Normandy. In late June 1944, the Speed Graphic with which Wigle took the photo was donated to the Fifth War Loan Drive. It was auctioned off over a radio network and brought $8,500,000 in War Bonds to the Community Savings Bank in Rochester, New York. After the war, Wigle returned to the *Detroit Times*.

BIBLIOGRAPHY

BOOKS

Adjutant General of New York State. *New York in the Spanish-American War.* Albany, N.Y.: James B. Lyon Co., 1900.

Army Times editors. *A History of the U.S. Signal Corps.* New York: G.P. Putnam's Sons, 1961.

Associated Press editors *The World in 1965.* New York: The Associated Press, 1965.

Berger, Meyer. *The Story of the New York Times 1851–1951.* New York: Simon & Schuster, 1951.

Bleiler, E.F., ed. *Alexander Gardner's Photographic Sketchbook of the Civil War.* New York: Dover Publishing Co., 1958.

Bourke-White, Margaret. *Portrait of Myself.* New York: Simon & Schuster, 1963.

Callahan, Sean. *The Photographs of Margaret Bourke-White.* New York: New York Graphic Society, 1972.

Capa, Cornell, and Karia Bhupendra, eds. *Robert Capa.* New York: Grossman Publishers, 1974.

Capa, Robert. *Images of War.* New York: Grossman Publishing Co., 1964.

Carnes, Cecil. *Jimmy Hare, News Photographer.* New York: Macmillan Co., 1940.

Chapelle, Dickey. *What's a Woman Doing Here?* New York: William Morrow and Co., 1961.

Cobb, Josephine. *Matthew B. Brady Photographic Gallery in Washington.* Washington, D.C.: Columbia History Society Records, 1954.

Duncan, David Douglas. *This Is War!* New York: Harper and Brothers, 1951.

Eder, J.M. *History of Photography.* New York: Columbia University Press, 1955.

Eichberg, Robert L., and Jacqueline Quadow. *Combat Photography.* Signal Corps Historical Project, 1947.

Encyclopedia of Photography. New York: Greystone Press. 1964.

Faber, John. *Great Moments in News Photography.* New York: Thomas Nelson and Sons, 1960.

Fabre, Maurice. *A History of Communication.* New York: Hawthorne Books, 1963.

Fairchild Instrument and Camera Company. *Focusing on Victory.* New York: Fairchild Co., 1944.

Favora, Anna, ed. *Robert Capa, A Monograph.* New York: Grossman Publishing Co., 1966.

Fawcett editors. *Famous Photographers Tell How.* Greenwich, Conn.: Fawcett Publishing Co., 1955.

Freidel, Frank. *Over There.* Boston: Little, Brown, and Co., 1964.

Frink, Maurice and Casey E. Barthelmess. *Photographer on an Army Mule.* Norman, Okla.: University of Oklahoma Press, 1965.

Gernsneim, Helmut. *The History of Photography.* London: Oxford University Press, 1955.

Giles, Willima. *"I Lug My Own Stuff and I Take No Favors."* National Observer Memorial Book on Dickey Chapelle. New York: Dow Jones Inc., 1966.

Gould, Lewis L., and Richard Greffe. *Photojournalist: The Career of Jimmy Hare.* Austin, Tex.: University of Texas Press, 1977.

Hansen, Harry, ed. *The World Almanac.* New York: New York World Telegram and the Sun, 1976.

Hemment, John C. *Cannon and Camera.* New York: D. Appleton and Co., 1899.

Hood, Robert E. *12 at War: Great Photographers Under Fire.* New York: Putnam, 1967.

Horan, James D. *Mathew Brady.* New York: Bonanza Books, 1955.

Hutton, Bud, and Andy Rooney. *The Story of the Stars and Stripes.* New York: Farran and Rinehart, 1946.

Joswick, Jerry, and Lawrence Keating. *Combat Cameraman.* Philadelphia: Chilton Co., 1961.

Kennerly, David Hume. *Shooter.* New York: Newsweek Books, 1979.

Leekley, Sheryl, and John Leekly. *Moments: The Pulitzer Prize Photographs.* New York: Crown, 1982.

Lewinski, Jorge. *The Camera at War.* New York: Simon & Schuster, 1980.

Life magazine editors. *Larry Burrows, Compassionate Photographer.* New York: Time-Life Books.

Maloney, Tom, ed. *U.S. Camera* (1951, 1953, 1954). New York: U.S. Camera Publishing Co., 1951, 1953, 1954.

Merideth, Roy. *Mr. Lincoln's Camera Man: Mathew Brady.* New York: Charles Scribner's Sons, 1951.

———. *Mr. Lincoln's Contemporaries.* New York: Charles Scribner's Sons, 1951.

Milhollen, Hirst D., and Milton Kaplan. *Divided We Fought.* New York: Macmillan, 1952.

Miller, Francis Trevelyan. *The Photographic History of the Civil War in Ten Volumes.* New York: The Review of Reviews Co., 1911.

Miller, Merle. *"Surprise Party at Eniwetck,"* The Best From Yank, The Army Weekly. Cleveland: The World Press, 1945.

Mott, Frank Buther. *A History of American Magazines 1885–1905.* Cambridge, Mass.: Harvard University Press, 1957.

Mydans, Carl. *More Than Meets The Eye.* New York: Harper and Brothers, 1959.

Newhall, Beaumont, and Nancy Newhall. *Masters of Photography.* New York: Bonanza Books, 1958.

Pollock, Peter. *The Picture Story of Photography.* New York: Abrams Publishing Co., 1958.

Reber, Samuel. *Manual of Photography.* Washington, D.C.: U.S. Government Printing Office, 1896.

Rothenstein, Sir John. *The World of Camera.* Garden City, N.Y.: Doubleday, 1965.

Sanborn, Herbert J. *Image of America.* Washington, D.C.: Library of Congress, U.S. Government Printing Office, 1957.

Sandburg, Carl. *Abraham Lincoln.* New York: Harcourt, Brace, and Co., 1954.

Schulman, Sammy. *"Where's Sammy?"* New York: Random House, 1943.

Steichen, Edward. *A Life in Photography.* Garden City, N.Y.: Doubleday, 1963.

———. *U.S. Navy War Photographers.* New York: U.S. Camera, 1964.

Stenger, Dr. Erich. *The History of Photography.* Easton, Penn.: Mack, 1939.

Taft, Robert. *Photography and the American Scene.* New York: Dover, 1938.

Vanderbilt, Paul. *Guide to the Special Collection of Prints and Photographs in the Library of Congress.* Washington, D.C.: Library of Congress, 1955.

Young, Gordon R., ed. *The Army Almanac.* Harrisbrurg, Penn.: The Telegraph Press, 1959.

PERIODICALS

Adam, Bill. "Combat in Korea," *U.S Camera.* 1954, p. 306.

Araham, Barbara. "Magnum, the First Ten Years," *Popular Photography.* September 1957, pp. 34–37.

American Journal of Photography. Vol. 4, 1861, p. 120.

"An Aviation Gun Camera," *Scientific American.* Vol. 116, March 31, 1917, p. 329.

Ansco News Release. February 21, 1961.

Anthony's Photographic Bulletin. December 1899.

A.P. Log. March 23, 1966.

———. April 30, 1966.

A.P. World Magazine. Vol. XX, no. 3, Winter 1965–66.

———. Vol. XXI, no. 1, Spring 1966.

Boling, Gerald R. "Men at War," *Our Navy Magazine.* Vol. 61, April 1966, p. 12.

Brown, Betty C. "The Third War of Horst Faas," *Popular Photography.* Vol. 58, no. 3, March 1966, p. 58.

Butler, E.K. "Invasion Pictures Took Long Preparations," *Editor and Publisher.* November 18, 1944, p. 16.

Buttner, Alexander. "Airship Photography in the War," *Photo-Era Magazine.* Vol. 36, March 1918, p. 108.

"The Camera at the Front," *Scientific American.* Vol. 117, November 24, 1917, p. 380.

Chapelle, Dickey. "You Must Know You Have Become Legend," *The National Observer.* June 28, 1965, p. 1.

Colling, James L. "He is a Very Strong-Willed Man, that Noel," *Editor and Publisher.* May 2, 1953, p. 48.

"Columbia University, an Armed Camp," *Scientific American*. Vol. 118, January 26, 1918, p. 87.

Coonley, J.F. "Pages from a Veteran's Notebook," *Wilson's Photographic Magazine* (NYC: Wilson Co.). Vol. 44, 1907, p. 106.

_____. "Photographic Reminiscences of the Late War, No. II," *Anthony's Photographic Bulletin* (NYC: Anthony and Co.). Vol. 13, 1882, p. 311.

Dawson, Albert K. "Photographing on the Firing Line," *Photo-Era Magazine*. Vol. 38, May 1917, p. 232.

Deepe, Beverly. "High Cost of Covering the War," *Overseas Press Club Bulletin*. Vol. 21, No. 9, March 6, 1966, p. 1.

Doherty, Robert J., Jr. "World War I," *Louisville Courier-Journal Magazine*. March 21, 1965, p. 14.

Downs, Bruce. "Assignment: Korea," *Popular Photography*. Vol. 29, no. 3, March 1951, p. 42.

Edom, Clifford C. "Photo-Propaganda, The History of Its Development," *Journalism Quarterly*. Vol. 24, no. 3, September 1947, p. 223.

Erwin, Ray. "Boston Globe Wins Pulitzer Prize Medal," *Editor and Publisher*. May 7, 1966, p. 59.

"Ex-Army Photog Wounded as AP Staffer In Vietnam," *National Press Photographer*. Vol. 21, no. 3, March 1966, p. 22.

Faas, Horst. "No Substitute for Being There—Faas on Vietnam," *National Press Photographer*. Vol. 21, no. 3, March 1966.

Frank Leslie's Illustrated Newspaper. Vol. 23, October 27, 1866, p. 219.

French, Wilfred A. "Aerial Fighting Cameras," *Photo-Era Magazine*. Vol. 41, November 1918, pp. 247, 249.

Friedman, Rich. "A Biographical Sketch," *Editor and Publisher*. May 6, 1944, p. 44.

_____. "Navy Has 10 Units in New Combat Photo Section," *Editor and Publisher*. April 17, 1943, p. 23.

_____. "Tribute to Photogs," *Editor and Publisher*. March 17, 1945, p. 40.

Harper's Weekly. Vol. 7, no. 359, November 14, 1863, pp. 534, 722.

Humphrey's Journal. Vol 13, 1861–62, pp. 21, 133.

Hunt, George P. "Tear Gas—A Problem for Photographers," *Life Magazine*. April 21, 1966, pp. 3.

Johnson, Harrison W. "The Development of Military Photographs," *The Signal Corps Bulletin*. No. 39, June 1927.

Louisville Courier-Journal. January 29, 1961, Magazine Section, p. 3.

McAfee, Lewis F. "How They Processed Ansco Color in Korea," *Popular Photography*. Vol. 30, no. 4, pp. 37–39.

National Intelligencer. May 23, 1863, p. 7.

New York Journal. July 7, 1898, p. 21.

_____. August 5, 1900, p. 1.

_____. February 7, 1903.

_____. July 7, 1949.

Overseas Press Club Bulletin. Vol. 21, no. 16, April 23, 1966, p. 1.

Philadelphia Photographer. Vol. 3, 1866, pp. 239, 287, 313, 339, 367, 371.

Popular Photography. March 1966, p. 137.

Price, Jack. "Air Force Photo School," *Editor and Publisher*. August 14, 1943, p. 30.

_____. "A.P.'s Filan Wins Pulitzer Award with War Shot," *Editor and Publisher*. May 6, 1944, p. 44.

_____. "Bob Bryant Bows in After 3 Years of War," *Editor and Publisher*. May 5, 1945, p. 60.

_____. "Captain Wall, D-Day Hero, Tells of Normandy," *Editor and Publisher*. November 11, 1944, p. 46.

_____. "Death Always in Focus for 3 Camera Knights," *Editor and Publisher*. December 2, 1944, p. 46.

_____. "Editors, Poets, Acclaim Rosenthal Iwo Photo," *Editor and Publisher*. March 17, 1945, p. 60.

_____. "Goldstein, INP Photographer, Back from African Front," *Editor and Publisher*. February 27, 1943, p. 18.

_____. "How Rosenthal Got Flag Photo," *Editor and Publisher*. March 10, 1945, p. 12.

_____. "Jap Bomb Fragment Hits Camera in Widdis's Hands," *Editor and Publisher*. September 19, 1942, p. 12.

_____. "Marine Newsman Made History at Tarawa," *Editor and Publisher*. December 11, 1943, p. 37.

_____. "Navy Plans Help Cameramen in Speedy Coverage on Iwo," *Editor and Publisher*. February 24, 1945, p. 7.

_____. "Photog's Woes in Pacific," *Editor and Publisher*. August 14, 1943, p. 30.

_____. "Picture Story of Invasion Well Planned," *Editor and Publisher*. October 7, 1944.

_____. "Pool Ends in Europe: Service Rivalry Due," *Editor and Publisher*. June 16, 1945, p. 34.

_____. "Rosenthal Describes His Technique on Iwo," *Editor and Publisher*. March 31, 1945, p. 34.

_____. "War Photos Need Luck Not Skill, Says Filan," *Editor and Publisher*. July 15, 1944, p. 28.

Publisher's Auxiliary. May 29, 1943, p. 6.

Resch, F.A. "Photo Coverage of the War by the Still Picture Pool," *Journalism Quarterly*. Vol. XX, No. 4, December 1943, p. 311.

Russell, A.J. "Photographic Reminiscences of the Late War, No. I," *Anthony's Photographic Bulletin* (NYC: Anthony and Co.). 1898, p. 171.

Schwalberg, Bob. "School for Combat Photographers," *Popular Photography*. Vol. 30, no. 6, June 1952, p. 46.

Scientific Monthly Magazine. Vol. 6, April 1918, p. 381.

Sheehan, Neil. "In Vietnam, War is Hell For Correspondants, Too," *Times Talk*. Vol. 18, no. 9, February 1966, p. 2.

Sondern, Frederick, Jr. "Dave Duncan and His Fighting Camera," *The Reader's Digest*. May 1951, p. 43.

Time magazine. June 10, 1966, p. 54.

Trabold, Edward R. "Counterattacking with a Camera," *Photographic Journal of America*. Vol. 56, 1919, p. 407.

Watson, Elmo Scott. "The Indian Wars and the Press," *Journalism Quarterly*. Vol. XVII, December 1940, p. 304.

Whitney, Allan, "The Role of the Camera in the Navy," *All Hands Magazine*. October 1963, pp. 2–6.

Wilson's Photographic Magazine. Vol. 34, 1899, p. 159.

_____. Vol. 44, 1907, p. 106.

DOCUMENTS

Historical Sketch of the Signal Corps (1860–1941). Eastern Signal Corps, U.S. Army, Fort Monmouth, N.J.

Library of Congress. *Civil War Photographs 1861–1865*. Washington, D.C.: Government Printing Office, 1961.

_____. *Document No. 5. List of Photographs and Negatives–Civil War*. Washington, D.C.: U.S. Govt. Printing Office, 1897.

National Archives. *A Preliminary Inventory of the Office of the Chief Signal Officer*. Washington, D.C.: U.S. Govt. Printing Office, 1961.

Navy Department News Release Dated December 4, 1943. Navy Department, Washington, D.C.

Navy Department. *Photographer's Mate 3*. Washington, D.C.: U.S. Govt. Printing Office, 1961.

Report of the Chief Signal Officer. Washington, D.C.: U.S. Govt. Printing Office, 1919.

A Tribute to Mathew B. Brady. Ansco Monograph, Binghamton, N.Y.: Ansco, 1961.

United States Army in the World War 1917–1919. Washington, D.C.: U.S. Govt. Printing Office, 1948. 15 volumes.

U.S. Army Signal Corps. *Exposure Under Fire: An Official History of Signal Corps Photography in the Luzon Operation*. April 25, 1945.

U.S. Army Technical Manual. TMll-6720-222-10.

U.S. Naval Institute Proceedings. "Combat Photography," by Sgt. Carl D. Ohman, October, 1944.

War Department Document. "Special List of World War I Photos," the Historical Section, the Army War College, Washington, D.C.

MAJOR DATES IN THE HISTORY OF WAR PHOTOGRAPHY

1847 An unknown daguerreotypist in Saltillo, Mexico makes the first photographic record of a battlefield, that of Buena Vista, Mexico.

1855 Englishman Roger Fenton becomes the world's first photographer to make pictures of troops in battle areas.

1856 The world's first military photography school is established in Chatham, England.

1859 Aerial photography of combat is used for the first time during the battle of Solferino, by soldiers under the command of Napoleon III.

1860 The French war minister orders that one officer in each army corps study photography.

1862 A photo course is instituted at the Military Cartography Institute in Vienna.

1866 On Sept. 14, Ridgeway Glover, of *Leslie's Illustrated Weekly*, is mortally wounded by Indians, becoming the first American photographer killed in a combat area.

1871 The French begin to teach photography at the Military School in Paris.

1871 The U.S. Army Signal Corps purchases its first camera.

1881 Sgt. George W. Rice, who in 1884 would starve to death while photographing an ill-fated Arctic expedition, becomes the first U.S. Army photographer.

1898 American military photographers become the first to use celluloid film rather than glass plates.

1899 In the Philippine Insurrection, U.S. Army photographer J.D. Saulsbury becomes the first American military photographer to be captured by the enemy. He is freed after about six months.

1900 Frances Johnson becomes the first American woman photographer assigned to combat areas.

1916 Ensign W.L. Richardson becomes the U.S. Navy's first photographer.

1917 An aerial "gun camera" is developed by the U.S. air service.

1917 The U.S. Army Signal Corps establishes its Aerial Photography School at Cornell University.

1918 The United States School of Photography (Land) is established at Columbia University.

1918 The U.S. Army School of Aerial Photography is established at Kodak Park, Rochester, New York.

1918 The first U.S. Navy photography school is established at the Naval Air Station, Miami, Florida.

1920 The navy's second school of photography is set up at Anacostia Naval Air Station, Maryland.

1941 The Signal School at Fort Monmouth, New Jersey, becomes home to the Army Still Photo School.

1942 The first school of photo interpretation for navy and marine personnel is established at Anacostia, Maryland.

1942 The Army Air Force School for Aerial Photography is set up at Lowry Field, Denver.

1943 Associated Press photographer Frank E. Noel wins the first Pulitzer Prize ever awarded for combat photography.

1943 The Signal Corps Pictorial Center is established at Long Island City, New York.

1944 The Naval School of Photography is set up at Pensacola, Florida.

1945 The Naval Photo Reconnaissance School is established at Whiting Field, Milton, Florida.

1965 In Vietnam, freelance photographer Dickey Chapelle becomes the first American woman photographer killed in action.

1993 The photo schools of the various armed services are combined into the Department of Defense Photo School in Pensacola, Florida.

1995 Classes in electronic imaging begin at the DOD Photo School in Pensacola, Florida.

PHOTOGRAPHY CREDITS

Endpapers (front): © David Hume Kennerly/UPI/Bettmann Archive

Endpapers (back): U.S. Army

Associated Press: 8, 40, 48–49, 51, 52, 55, 87 (left), 106, 131; © Eddie Adams: 95; © Brady Photographer: 22–23; © Robert Capa: 75; © Dickey Meyer Chapelle: 68, 106; © Max Desfor: 85; © David Douglas Duncan: 82; © Frank Filan: 62–63; © Horst Faas: 93, 94 left, 100, 102, 111; © Matt Franjola: 99 (right); © Alexander Gardner: 18; © Art Greenspan: 92; © Ronald L. Haeberle: 104; © Henri Huet: 101; © Christopher Morris: 118–119; © Huynh Thanh My: 99 (left); © Frank Noel: 61, 87 (right); © Joe Rosenthal: 60; © Huyhn Cong Ut: 109

Bettmann Archive: 9, 10, 25, 31, 44–45

Brady Photographer: 12, 16, 27; Library of Congress: 13, 14; Alexander Gardner/U.S. Army; National Archives/U.S. Army: 26, 28–29; U.S. Army: 19

Courtesy Cornell Capa: 77

© J.C.H. Grabill/Courtesy Museum of New Mexico/Negative 101935: 33

© Stan Grossfeld/Boston Globe: 118

Library of Congress: 10–11, 15, 68; Photo attributed to George Barnard: 20–21; William Dinwiddie: 38–39; John Hemment: 34

© Tomas Muscionico/Contact Press Images: 117

National Archives: 50; Timothy O'Sullivan/U.S. War Department: 24

George Silk, *Life* magazine/© Time, Inc.: 59

Reuters/Bettmann: © Will Burgess: 116; Andy Clark: 121; © Santiago Lyon: 120; © Mike Marcuss: 124; © Frederic Neema: 126–127; © Charles Platiau: 123, 125; © Claude Salhani: 122–123

Smithsonian Institution: 32

UPI/Bettmann: 72, 113; © David Hume Kennerly: 103; © Toshio Sakai: 96–97; © Kyoichi Sawada: 94 (right), 98, 105, 108; © Dana Stone: 107, 112

U.S. Air Force: 64; George R. Caron: 80

U.S. Army: 30, 35, 36, 37, 46, 47, 54, 65, 66–67, 70, 83, 84; Harry W. Chadwick: 41; Al Chang: 89; Courtesy of Eastman Kodak Press Department: 53; James Hare: 42–43; Frances Benjamin Johnston: 44; Herman Wall: 76

U.S. Marine Corps: 57, 69, 73; M.J. Bolhower: 88; J. Fabian: 56; Walter Frank: 90–91; Kleins: 80–81; Moorejohn: 128

U.S. Navy: 70–71, 79; Jean C. Cote: 87 (left); 110; D.S. Dodd: 115

INDEX